Germany – It's More Than Bratwurst & Weißbier

A Young Family Exploring a New Life in Germany

Martin D. Barber

Contents

Introduction

Life in the late 1980s and early 1990s

PICKING UP pen and paper, or my laptop, almost thirty years after the events that led me and my family to move to Germany, provided me with some wonderful memories. I decided to sit down and go through just how the sequence of events happened, as well as how we ended up over a thousand miles away from our home town of Sudbury in Suffolk.

It wasn't quite *Auf Wiedersehen Pet*, where several English construction workers leave the UK to search for employment overseas. This was more of a survival dream to keep our heads above the parapet, with the family finances as well as company finances. I ran a local roofing company at the time. Trying as hard as I could to rebuild my failing career at such an early age, I had suffered huge losses when a local building company in Ipswich collapsed, leaving me and my business with a hole in the bank so deep that I really didn't know where to turn or who to ask for help.

Looking back now, I know I pushed the boundaries of love and commitment of both my wife and family. I must have driven my family and loved ones to the very limit with the events described in this book, but we eventually came through it somehow. Looking back, the whole adventure has given me, my wife Vanessa and all three of our sons, Lee, Jake and Sam, a very colourful and adventurous outlook on life that we all still carry with us to this day. We lived these events through the early to mid-1990s and they have helped to mould us into the people we are today.

I should add here that, out of courtesy, I've changed the name of some of the friends and characters along the journey for reasons I'm sure you will understand.

Please enjoy the memories, the events and challenges throughout our early years in Germany. If nothing else, this book really does prove, as I've often said to all three of my sons throughout their lives:

Follow your dreams; it's dreams that
make you happy in life.

Chapter 1

Christmas 1993

M Y GOOD friend and workmate Steve arrived on time to collect me on 26 December 1993. Yes, it was Boxing Day, and we were on our way to collect a long-wheelbase 7-tonne truck from a local hire firm. It was a forty-five-minute journey on a pretty miserable Sunday evening, pouring with rain.

We collected the truck at 7pm as planned and I headed back to my house in the village of Glemsford, just outside Sudbury, in readiness to load up first thing in the morning. I thanked Steve and we made our arrangements to meet up on Tuesday for the trip to southern Germany.

It was still raining at 7am on the Monday morning when my friends Dave and Harry arrived to help load all our furniture into the truck. Everything was boxed and ready to go, and all I could hope was that the vehicle was large enough to get the job done.

Vanessa was stressing about all the furniture and boxes that needed to be put into the truck, as well as being nervous at the same time about just what she had let herself and our children in for with the coming adventure.

We put everything we couldn't get in the truck into one of the bedrooms, placed locks on the door, and left this stuff to be stored until we returned. Our house was to be rented out to the local RAF Mildenhall base, which primarily supports the US Air Force, for one of their senior families to live in while we were away. It all seemed like a well-planned military operation, but without Vanessa and her mother getting most of this move organised while I was away working, we would never have been able to get it done in the short time that I had been back in the UK over this Christmas period.

By 2pm the truck was loaded, and I headed over to my in-laws, where I would be staying with Vanessa and the children overnight. Steve arrived at 4am on the Tuesday, and we jumped into the truck and said our goodbyes to Vanessa and the boys, then headed to Dover to get the move underway.

Steve is a great guy and a lot of fun to be around. We had been working together at the same roofing company for just over twelve months in southern Germany. He had joined me and the small troop of guys who were working for me there, and we lived and worked together, so we all had to get on or trouble would rise in the camp, as inevitably it did from time to time.

I had taken on the role of capo, or leader, of the troop as I was the one with some business history. All the guys worked for me and I took a very small percentage of their earnings to cover the costs of invoicing and the few hours each week I spent sorting out their payments and making sure they were all paid on time. I can tell you it wasn't an easy task.

You may ask why I was working in Germany. I had no choice really; in fact, it was a necessity, as eighteen months earlier I had lost a huge amount of money when a local building company in Ipswich had closed down overnight. It had gone into administration, leaving me and Vanessa with a huge hole in our finances and struggling to sort out the mess we found ourselves in.

Steve and I arrived at Dover just after 6.30am, and the customs inspectors pulled us over for a look inside the truck. They wanted to know what we were doing, and this is when I made my first mistake of the journey.

The officer asked, 'Do you have any knives on board?'

I jokingly replied, 'Yeah, loads. I've got all my kitchen cutlery in there somewhere.'

This wasn't taken as the jovial response I had hoped and intended it to be. I was ordered to turn out all the contents of the truck for inspection. Steve was fuming, most of his anger aimed at me for being such a fool and getting lippy with the customs officer. Mind you, my anger was aimed at the officer, as he knew only too well what I had meant. He was obviously bored as he was on the early morning shift on a Christmas week. No nights out for him!

After two hours the officer walked back to the two of us. We had just about finished emptying the truck, swearing every time he came into eyeshot. He took no more than thirty seconds to look over the contents with nothing more than a lazy eye. He looked at the contents laid all over the floor, as well as what we were still taking out of the truck, then instructed us to pack it all back and be on our way as soon as possible as we were taking up valuable space in the depot.

Steve was even more furious now. We knew this guy had just been having a good laugh at our expense, keeping him amused during that long boring morning, even if I had started the damn problem with my idiotic comment.

By 11am we were safely on the ferry to Calais, albeit three hours late now. It was straight into the café for me to get us breakfast and a strong cup of coffee. It was the first time we'd had chance to eat all morning.

The crossing was calm and uneventful, and before we knew it, we were winding our watches forward an hour to European time, then hitting the road to the south of France. We were heading for the south-eastern city of Strasbourg, on the border with Germany and the famous Black Forest region. It was a seven-hour journey on the first section as we could only travel at 80 kph, as the truck had a speed limiter fitted. We could go faster when we were driving downhill, but that didn't happen too often.

We had both made this journey several times over the past year, heading back for either a week at home to visit our families and loved ones, or sometimes just for a short weekend. I couldn't afford the luxury of too much time off work as I had debts to pay, and every penny I was earning had been sent back to Vanessa to juggle our debts. We had repayment plans in place after the huge loss we had taken on. She was doing a great job of holding the fort though, which wasn't easy with me being a thousand miles away. I needed to work, work and work even more to get the money we needed to get ourselves out of the mess we had found ourselves in.

Seven hours and nearly a thousand kilometres later we were coming off the toll roads in France at Brumath, heading north for a short journey to Haguenau, before weaving our way east to cross the German border. We crossed over the Rhine at one of its widest points, the Rheinknie Alter Kopfgrund. To cross the river here there's a series of bridges and traffic lights that cross sections of the river, as well as a huge island in the middle. The bridges criss-cross the Rhine before taking you to the state of Baden-Württemberg in southern Germany.

By now, we had been travelling for fourteen hours in all, changing drivers every two hours. It was a slow hard slog of a journey, but thankfully it had been dry, with good road conditions, as well as being quiet on the roads. We headed north on the main autobahn, then around the outskirts of the city of Karlsruhe.

Moving on, we could smell the home stretch coming close as we picked up the A8 autobahn heading east past Pforzheim, then skirting the major city of Stuttgart. We had one last stop at the services close to Stuttgart airport to pick up some essential provisions for the evening before heading to where we would be staying, which was at Steve's apartment in the centre of Reutlingen.

Prior to this move, I had been living with Steve at his apartment, but with my family finally joining me, I had found a new place to live, though still in Reutlingen, the city we would be calling home for the foreseeable future.

We arrived just before midnight, parked the truck safely and headed into Steve's place. It was cold – bloody cold – minus nine outside and a light dusting of snow covering the city. But for now it was time for a well-earned beer, an oven pizza, then hit the sack ready for another crazy day tomorrow.

We were both up by 7am the following morning. It was still dark outside. We discussed what time to get to the other side of the city to empty the van and agreed that it needed to be done in daylight as the entrance road to my new apartment was very narrow. There were also always a lot of parked cars around the property, and the last thing I wanted was to hit a parked car before I even got to know my new neighbours!

By 8.30am we were reversing the truck up Behring Strasse, at the foot of the Achalm, a small mountain 600 metres above sea level, right in the middle of the city. It dominates the skyline of Reutlingen. This was to be our new family home, but first we needed to unload the truck and get all the beds assembled and made up for when we all arrived back. I didn't want to be doing this when I returned with the family after a long journey, especially with three tired boys from a full day's travelling.

So, we got the beds in first, and I started to assemble them as Steve carried on moving in all he could on his own. By 11.30am I had finished, and two hours later the house was full of all our furniture. All I needed to do now was to pop to the local DIY shop to pick up some light bulbs, as all the light fittings had been left empty. All I could think was that things must have been really tight for the last people living here if they needed to take their light bulbs with them.

Finally, by 4pm we were all finished and were left with a choice to make: Do we get our heads down or do we just get back to Calais as soon as possible and get home? We decided on the latter and journeyed back the way we had come. Again, it was an uneventful journey, but the temperature was getting colder as we headed north through France.

We arrived at Calais in the early hours of the morning and managed to get the 6am ferry back to Dover. It had been a very quick turnaround, just forty-eight hours, and by the time we were back in the UK and I had dropped the truck off and taken Steve home, I hit the pillow of my temporary bed at the in-laws' house at 1pm the following afternoon, absolutely shattered. I had been on the go for almost thirty-six hours, but even as young as I was then, my body was feeling it.

It was now Thursday, 30 December and we were due to drive to Germany in a week's time as a family, so for the next few days we were being entertained by Brian (known to us as Jock) and Diane, Vanessa's parents, as well as visiting all the aunties and grandparents for a final farewell before we headed off on our German adventure.

It was only years later that I realised what a daunting period this was for Vanessa's parents, as at that time there were no mobile phones. In addition, we didn't have, indeed couldn't actually afford, a landline when we arrived in Germany either. The only form of contact for the family was to write letters, then arrange to have a weekly call from a phone box to catch up and tell everyone how we were getting on. Not ideal, but for me it was my dream come true as Vanessa and the boys were going to be joining me and we would be a family once again.

New Year came and went and on Wednesday, 5 January 1994 we were all packing ourselves into the 1973 BMW 5 series car that I had only had for two months, a car that I hoped would get us to Reutlingen. Lee, my eldest at seven years old, fell straight to sleep once he was in the car, while the twins, Jake and Sam, who were five years old, were loving the adventure of getting up at 3.30am, having an early breakfast and heading off to a new country. Not that any of the boys could really understand exactly what was happening, and if I'm honest even I didn't fully understand the enormity of what we were doing.

Vanessa and I had been childhood sweethearts since we were sixteen and we married at eighteen. Now at twenty-five years old neither of us really understood what we were doing, moving to the other side of Europe. The journey for me, though, was for us to start over again, and to become a family once more after such a bad two years since we had got into so much debt. I wanted us to enjoy each other and the boys as well as start to enjoy our life together.

Steve arrived at 4am to drive down with us as he had a nearly new BMW cabriolet, and he was my 'get out of jail' if we broke down on the way. At least he could get help and ensure we weren't stranded. By 4.30am we were on our way. Vanessa's parents were tearful, so was Vanessa, but the twins were bouncing off the car roof with excitement. Lee, as I said, was fast asleep.

Arriving in Calais at 9.30am, I took the lead as Steve followed. We stopped for a coffee and breakfast an hour later, giving the opportunity for the boys to spend a penny. Lee then jumped in with Steve, which was nice for him to have some special time in Steve's posh car. We headed out on the same route that Steve and I had taken a week previously with the furniture, but this time it was a quicker journey as we weren't restricted on our speed.

By the time we entered Germany over the River Rhine it was a little after 4pm. Lee jumped back into my car as we stopped at the Pforzheim services near Stuttgart, and I told Steve to head off so he could get home. I'm sure he was very bored, as he could have driven faster in his flashy car and would have been home two hours ago.

Finally, we were on our own, and we arrived at our new home just after 8pm. The boys were shattered but also very excited to be in what was to be their new home. Vanessa helped them get ready for bed and I emptied the car, getting all our luggage and travel bits in.

This was it; the boys were asleep within twenty minutes after some giggling and excited laughing, and Vanessa and I were sitting alone in what looked like a bombed-out apartment. Furniture and boxes were strewn everywhere, our bed being the only thing that we were able to sit on. I could see she was already having second thoughts. I knew this had to work for her as well as the boys. I also knew my job was to make it work for them as I didn't want her and the boys yearning to return to the UK. I needed her to fall in love with the culture and lifestyle I had found, to fulfil my hope for us to become a family once again.

Chapter 2

School, Kindergarten and the Volksschule

IT WAS Thursday morning and our first day in our new home. The boys were up and bouncing on their beds by 6.30am, all shouting and playing with so much excitement. I was just shattered, having driven more than 3,000 miles in just over a week, and was in need of a lie in, but I knew I wasn't going to get it.

We had a few provisions that we had brought with us in a cool bag, such as milk, cheese and butter, so we could make some breakfast, which ended up as cheese sandwiches and a cup of tea. We couldn't even have toasties as we hadn't got any European plugs to change the toaster plug. So, that was the first thing added to the to-do list, which over the coming days just kept growing.

We decided to get wrapped up warm against the cold outside and take a walk into the city. It was minus two with very little wind, so relatively warm for the time of year here. Once everyone was ready, off we went for our route march to the city centre, trying to find a way through the back roads from where we lived into the shopping areas of Reutlingen. After a few wrong turns, we finally arrived in the centre.

Reutlingen has a very long high street with all the major shops, as well as several smaller streets leading off that have small artisan shops and designer clothing stores. The city was known as the gold city of Germany during the 1980s and 90s, producing more millionaires than any other region in the country; for example, Willi Betts, who is one of Reutlingen's most famous patrons and was CEO of Europe's largest transport company. I can remember hearing about when he signed a deal directly with Mercedes-Benz for three thousand five hundred new trucks; that's some order!

The boys, although a little cold, were loving their new surroundings, and Vanessa was too. There was a real enjoyment walking through the city that first morning. Families were out enjoying the last few days of their Christmas and New Year holidays before work started again on the coming Monday. As an indulgence on the first day we headed into McDonalds to treat the boys to a cheeseburger and milkshake.

On our way back home, I pointed out to Vanessa the new school Lee would be attending, which was a fifteen-minute walk from our house. It was enormous compared to the village school he had just left back in the UK, which had fewer than a hundred pupils.

Before returning to the UK before Christmas, I had been into the school to meet the principal and was introduced to Lee's new teacher, Frau Hilderbrand. I had a really good chat with her, and she was very excited about having Lee join her class. She explained that he would be in her class for the next year and a half and that she would keep a very close eye on him, as at that time he obviously spoke no German at all. She reassured me that he would very quickly learn the language and told me that she would be in touch if she thought there were any problems after he had started.

Just around the corner from Behring Strasse and our new home was the kindergarten that the twins would be attending. Again, I had already paid a visit to meet the principal, Frau Schovel. She too was a lovely lady, also extremely excited to have two young English children joining her. I realised that Vanessa was very nervous about the boys joining the schools as she only had my word that everything would be okay for them.

Money at this time was still very tight, and we were constantly counting every penny (in this case pfennig), especially on our arrival, as I hadn't worked now for two weeks due to the Christmas break period. However, we enjoyed a lovely first weekend, and I wasn't going to be working on the first Monday back, to ensure the boys got to their schools okay and to help Vanessa cope with everything in her new German life too.

On the Monday, Lee was fine, with no tears at all when we dropped him off, but Vanessa was a little tearful as we walked back home, leaving him for the whole three hours he would be at school that first day. Jake and Sam started one hour after Lee, so we had time to get home and have a coffee before walking the 100 metres to their new school. Both the boys were very quiet, and it would take several weeks before they started to adapt to their new language and their new teachers.

Neither wanted to be left that day and this really did affect Vanessa. We walked back home and found that we could see the children playing in the kindergarten from our apartment so that was reassuring for her. And at least they could play, even if they couldn't yet communicate with their new friends.

At noon I walked down to Lee's school and collected him. I had previously promised him that if he was good on his first day at school, we would go to the bakery close by to meet Steve for a cake of Lee's choice. He didn't need reminding as he came running out of school, shouting goodbye in English to his new school friends, and immediately asking whether we were still going for cake.

Steve had been at work all morning, but he had arranged to meet me and Lee for a coffee in his lunch hour. This really did help Lee on his first day in this new environment. Lee loved Steve, who made him laugh all the time, which for me was a real positive too, with all the changes in Lee's life at that moment.

Lee chose an Americana for his cake, a flat sponge cake, saucer-shaped, about 2 to 3 centimetres thick, with a covering of white and dark chocolate over the top. He ate the whole thing and I could see then that his first day had been a memorable one as well as enjoyable, especially the cake.

We headed back home, and it was soon time to pop next door to the kindergarten to collect Jake and Sam. They were only too pleased to see us. As I said, this was going to be a work in progress, introducing them into this new way of life. They weren't going to be as easy as Lee to integrate.

Later that afternoon we all walked once again into the city to see what was available for Vanessa in the local volkshochschule, a school set up by the German state as a non-profit-making adult education school. As we were at the start of January, Vanessa would only have to wait two weeks before the start of the next beginners' course for the German language, so she enrolled straight away.

It had been a very busy first day, with all the boys being thrown into the deep end of German schooling as well as Vanessa signing up for her own schooling. Me, well I was just over the moon that I had my family around me once again. I knew the coming weeks were definitely not going to be easy, and both Vanessa and I had to learn to live together again after almost eighteen months apart.

I had been here on my own in Germany earning the sort of money that I had no chance of earning in the current climate back in the UK. If you're wondering why Germany was so busy for construction workers, just remember this was the aftermath and demise of the old Eastern Bloc, with East and West Germany having now unified. With so much infrastructure to be put in place and the need for so much construction work, new roads, housing, etc., it was a mammoth task. It saw workers from all over Europe flocking into Germany to help with the rebuilding of their country. I was one of those guys.

Although we weren't out of debt yet, we were now very close. Another six to twelve months and we could finally start to enjoy the hours I had been working so hard and so long for. We would be able to spoil ourselves a little … well that was the plan anyway.

Early that evening we had a knock at the door, and I opened it to be confronted by a lovely bubbly lady who spoke perfect English, albeit with a real American accent.

'Hi guys,' she bellowed out with a huge smile all over her face. 'We have just popped in to welcome you to the Behring Strasse.' I then noticed what I took to be her son hanging on to her side. He could only have been about three years old but he smiled, although he appeared to be very shy.

The woman, who introduced herself as Annie, then went on to explain that she lived two floors above us. Her mother would be visiting later and she would bring her down to meet us too.

I was getting a little lost in all the explanations of who, what and why, and Vanessa soon joined me to push me out of the way and invite Annie and her son Karl into the apartment. Vanessa apologised for my rudeness in not inviting them in, and I was instructed to go into the kitchen to make tea while Vanessa got to know Annie better.

I soon learned that Annie was half English, her father being from the UK, and he had married her German mother. The American accent came from the fact that she was married to an American army guy who was stationed in Germany but was living on base over 200 kilometres away near Nuremburg and who came home only for weekends. After an hour or so, Annie popped back up to her home and assured us she would return later with her mother.

When we met her mother later, she was an absolute darling. As soon as I opened the door, she stood there next to Annie and Karl with a huge friendly smile. She gently wished us a very warm welcome to Germany and Behring Strasse, as well as informing me that her name was Gabrielle, or Gaby for short, she insisted. But from that first day onwards she would always be known as 'Mum' to me.

I invited everyone in, having learned my lesson from earlier about not standing on the doorstep, and we all sat chatting about how we had ended up here in Reutlingen, as well as how Gaby ended up married to an Englishman. They also explained that he had died several years ago and she was a widow. Gaby also spoke fantastic English, with just a hint of a German accent, but only if you were really listening hard.

I could tell straight away that we had just found some great new friends that would help us settle in. Vanessa had someone in Annie just upstairs who she could have a coffee with and do what women do … talk, talk and talk some more. But, most importantly, she had a friend to help her through the long days while I was out working in this foreign land.

A short while later there was another knock at the door. This time there appeared to be a whole household standing in front of me when I opened the door. As a lady started to speak to me in German, explaining who she was and who the other people were, Annie popped her head round the corner and started a conversation with the new visitors. I was nothing but a spectator to the conversation, my German skills at this time, I admit, being extremely limited. I did, however, recognise one person in Franz, a guy I had met in late November while hunting high and low throughout the city for an apartment to rent. He was the person who had helped me to rent this apartment, and to my amazement I now found out that he was Gaby's brother, Annie's uncle. What a small world.

Standing next to Franz was his wife Elsbeth, as well as his daughter Sabine, who we found out was our next-door neighbour, along her husband Johannes, their two-year-old daughter Madeline and seven-year-old son Gernold.

I invited everyone in, as well as the crate of beer that came with Johannes and the bottle of schnapps that came with Franz. We were all introduced to each other, and what soon became apparent was that only Annie and Gaby spoke English, and that everyone else had similar or worse English skills than our German.

Overall, this proved to be a great confidence booster for Vanessa, who had no German at all. Putting this aside, we spent a great couple of hours chatting with the added help of sign language, as well as a few words from each of our mother tongues, Annie and Gaby translating as quickly as possible as we all became acquainted. Some great friendships started on that night, in only our first week in Germany.

Franz ran his insurance brokerage in the town and he was our landlord too. He owned the house and rented the six apartments out. Sabine had a beauty parlour local to us, aided by her mother Elsbeth, while Johannes was a self-employed builder who could turn his hand to almost anything and everything that came his way. Madeline was a sweet little blonde-haired angel who just loved to live in her own little dream world. Gernold was the same age as Lee, and the two boys wasted no time becoming the very best of friends from that day onwards. Looking back, as a family we owe so much to Gernold for helping both me and Vanessa to learn German ... well he was one of the many helpers.

During the discussions we were informed that we had a middle-aged lady who lived alone directly above us – Frau Brandt. Opposite her, and above Sabine and Johannes, were two elderly ladies, Frau Schmitt and Frau Elbster, who turned out to be the sweetest of ladies. Above them, lived Annie and Karl, and the last of the apartments that was opposite Annie and Karl on the top floor was currently unoccupied. It wasn't long before we would all become very good friends in the coming weeks and months.

We also learned that Franz was finishing off one more small studio apartment below our ground floor apartment, constructed in a small section of the cellar, but that was work in progress and totally unhabitable at that time.

Now we had great friends on the doorstep and Vanessa had met the family next door, who had children the same age as ours, which would be a priceless friendship for our time here in Germany. Upstairs, Annie was always on hand to help translate letters, help with the local registration and everything else we would throw at her. Life already looked as if it would be great here in our small apartment, where we were surrounded by new friends, and I had guaranteed work. I really did want for nothing. Life was on the up and we were once again a family living together.

Chapter 3

Franz – My New Best Buddy

WHEN YOU'RE self-employed and mainly working outside in the elements, winter isn't too bad back in the UK. Rain is something you get used to, being British, as well as the constant wind that's always blowing around you. Here in Reutlingen there's no wind to worry about in winter or summer, though. Being nearly a thousand kilometres from any coastline it's quite sheltered.

I also had the assurance from my employers that I would be working no more than thirty minutes from their office, so all my working time would be, in their words, very local. This was a real must, having brought Vanessa and the boys to Germany so we could be together. However, the one thing I hadn't envisaged was the problem of snow and ice. The previous year I had lost little time to the weather through the winter months, so I just expected that this year would be the same. How wrong I was.

My first two weeks back in work were fine, the temperature was down to minus five on a bad day, but with no wind to contend with and blue skies, it was quite manageable, so I wasn't losing any working time at all. We still had debts to repay and just having got through Christmas and New Year, as well as the time and money spent moving to Germany, there was only small change left in the bank.

Then by the last week of January things got worse. We had a snowfall of 10 to 12 centimetres overnight, and although the roads were still clear when I arrived at work, we were informed that we had to wait until the following morning to work as the forecast was for more snow during that day.

One day lost is no major problem, so I returned home and spent some time helping Vanessa tidy the apartment, as we still had decorating to do and I needed to put new light fittings in. I also had to find a cheap solution to get a work surface installed to one side of the long and narrow galley kitchen. So, we decided the work surface was my task for the day and I set off to the local DIY centre to find the cheapest solution.

The snow was falling again by now, although there was only a centimetre or two of fresh snow on the roads. However, it was starting to come down like I had never seen before, with flakes the size of fifty pence pieces. So, by the time I had spent almost an hour mooching around the DIY centre and purchasing the materials there was another 10 to 12 centimetres of snow on the ground.

I strapped the materials on to the roof rack and gingerly made my way home. As winter tyres weren't compulsory at the time, everyone was driving very cautiously. I arrived home at approximately 10.45am and was surprised to find that the children were home too. Apparently, when the snow becomes too much in any one day, public transport is affected, and if temperatures fall below minus ten, the schools just shut down and all children are sent home. This is fine if you're aware of the education rules, but we were newbies, so Vanessa had the shock of her life when the twins suddenly turned up from kindergarten, closely followed by Lee from his school. He had walked home with Gernold from next door, sent home on 'winterfrei', the name given to the schools closing when these conditions are upon us.

Having had this explained to us by Annie, I set about building the kitchen work surface, aided now by my two little helpers, Jake and Sam, with Lee having gone to Gernold's house to play for the rest of the day.

Little did I know that this would be the first of many days at home. Winter had set in, and over the next few days we had sporadic snow showers. It was nothing of great depth, but the temperatures hovered between minus five and minus twelve. The snow was being cleared from the roads daily by the local authority, but the roofs were full of snow, up to 40 centimetres now, and it was going nowhere.

We tried to put a brave face on it. Losing one day was fine, but losing a week was extremely bad news. As we entered the second week of bad weather, Vanessa and I were extremely worried, as our very small emergency fund was already teetering on empty.

On my second Monday at home I was again clearing the snow from the entrance to the house when Franz arrived and parked his car. He looked agitated and somewhat stressed as he hurried into his daughter's apartment.

Within a minute he was back out and calling to me, 'Martin, ich brauche deine hilfe.' (Martin, I need your help.) My German wasn't great but I could just about work out that he wanted me to go with him for some reason, so we jumped into his car. I listened intently to him talking to me, most probably telling me why and where we were heading out in his car, but I had absolutely no idea what he was talking about or where we were going.

A few minutes later we arrived at his office and home. He had a large detached house on one of the main roads leading away from the town, and his office was on the ground floor. He and Elsbeth lived on the two floors above. As he parked the car, I could already see what the problem was. Elsbeth had her own car and she had reversed out of the driveway, but the car had decided to slide all the way over to the other side of the road and into the side of another vehicle. With snow and ice all over the road, as well as some cars having been parked for several days in the same place at the side of the road, the actual width of the road was much narrower than it would normally be.

Franz had been unable to move the car and Elsbeth had gone into meltdown and was in hysterics. Franz was giving some very sharp instructions to her and she in turn was screaming back at him what I can only think were obscenities. If anyone else had witnessed it I'm sure they would have intervened, but as I spoke little to no German all I could do was look on and wonder what the hell I was doing here.

Ranting and raving over, Franz started with his best German-English hand signals and I returned with my best English-German response. Between the two of us, we hooked up Elsbeth's car to Franz's large estate vehicle and managed to pull her car free so that Franz could fit a set of snow chains and reverse the car back on to the driveway.

Franz, again in his best sign language, signalled to me with a shovelling action, wanting me to help clear his drive and the road around his house. By this time, I was thinking to myself that maybe I should just take up sign language, as I seemed to have a natural talent for understanding it.

Two hours later we had moved the snow and ice. Franz had popped out for thirty minutes and returned with some rock salt. He had tried to explain why he was going out, but I hadn't understood. All I could do was nod my head, smile and keep saying, 'Ja, ja,' with the occasional thumbs up. At least it made me feel as if I was in the conversation, but Franz must have thought I was just another bloody foreigner with no idea.

Anyway, two hours later the road was clear as well as his driveway and the whole area salted to prevent further incident. Franz then wrote a small note, placed it on the windscreen of the car Elsbeth had slid into and, once we had finished, I was invited in for what I hoped would be a hot drink to warm up.

We walked through the office at the front of the property, the same office I had first met Franz in when I came to look at the apartment back in November the previous year. We entered a small kitchen area that I presumed belonged to his working office. Franz asked, 'Drink?' and I was still thinking of a hot cuppa, so I said 'ja' followed once again by that great international thumbs-up sign.

Coffee was obviously not on offer, nor was a cup of tea. Franz opened the fridge and out came two beers. Bottle tops were quickly removed and Franz gave a swift 'prost' to toast the morning's work.

On the third or fourth beer Franz dug into his pocket and pulled out a DM100 note (the Euro was but a dream away at the time) and handed it to me to thank me for helping him. I objected to being paid, but with no real spoken German and him having no English, all he said was 'ja' followed by a little thumbs up and wry smile as he slipped the note into my hand.

He turned back to the fridge and opened another two beers, placing them on the table, before putting a bottle of Williams pear schnapps alongside them. The time was now getting on for 1pm and I would almost certainly have been missed at home by now, as all I had gone out to do was clear the snow from our entrance at 8.30am. I had been gone for over four hours and by now was starting to slur my words.

However, my German seemed to be improving with each beer. Well, to me it was, and Franz was also getting better at English as we both talked waffle and drank some more. The schnapps was now coming in small glasses filled to the brim, and it was clear to me that Franz was obviously no beginner to this drinking during the day. The glasses were filled every twenty minutes or so, until by 3pm I had to make my excuses and apologies as I needed to go home.

If I'm honest, I felt a little queasy in Franz's house but thought that I had handled myself quite well, considering I wasn't really much of a drinker. It wasn't until I had finally convinced Franz I would walk and that he wasn't driving me home that I opened the office door and hit the fresh, cold, in fact very cold air. I managed to turn the corner out of his driveway before I had to hold on to the first lamppost nearby, followed by the neighbour's fence. I just had to hold on to steady myself. I really was in an extremely bad way, and from leaving Franz's place it took me over an hour to do the ten-minute walk home, before arriving extremely drunk and frozen stiff. Here I was met by an exceptionally unwelcoming Vanessa at the front door as I rang the bell to be let in.

I can't remember too much after the door opening, apart from a stern look from Vanessa and the three boys all shouting and screaming for daddy. Once the warmth of the apartment had engulfed me, I sat down on the sofa to ponder on my new friend Franz and the first DM100 I had earned in over a week.

It wasn't until the following morning that the memory of what had happened came back as, apparently, I had just drifted off to sleep the evening before, so Vanessa had left me there on the sofa for the night to sleep it off.

Franz, my new buddy, was to become a very good source of income as well as an extremely good friend to all of us during our time in Germany. But some of the jobs he had for me really were beyond the call of any normal person's duty, and each job was also accompanied by a drink or two. In time, I would try my best to avoid these sessions, but try as I might, eventually Franz always got his way.

Chapter 4

Fasching on the Schwäbische Alb

L IKE MOST of you reading the word 'Fasching', I had absolutely no idea what this was. Everyone in the company I worked for and all my new neighbours were talking about this celebration for weeks ahead, leading up to 'Weiberfastnacht', which is the last Thursday before Ash Wednesday. This is the night when celebrations of Fasching, or Karneval as it's also known in Reutlingen, start.

This celebration is the equivalent of Mardi Gras and dates back many hundreds of years. It's a time for feasting, drinking, fancy dress parades and parties, not forgetting the crazy masks and costumes worn on the parades by the partygoers. Everyone lets their hair down just before the fasting time of Lent. It's also a celebration to chase away those winter demons.

Annie had told us all about the Fasching carnival on the Schwäbische Alb, which was to be on the first and second Saturdays of February. She explained in some detail what the celebration is all about, and after her invitation to show us the celebrations in Engstingen, a small village only about 17 kilometres from our home, how could we refuse? We came here to be a family, here we were in this foreign country and it was the experiences of the Germanic cultures that we were now to be soaking up.

Lee's pal Gernold was to come with us, as they had become real best friends already, so along with Annie we left at around 10am. It was an easy drive from Reutlingen, straight through the city, then up the wall of stone called the Schwäbische Alb, which rises over 200 metres. Engstingen is only a fifteen-minute drive from the top of the climb and we were soon entering the village and managed to park up with little trouble.

Gernold and Lee were both extremely excited about the parade that would come within the hour. I'm sure Lee was excited purely because Gernold was, as he had never experienced anything like this back in the UK.

Annie led us to the main high street through the village, and we managed to find a shop front that had a wide and high step that the children could stand on for a good view. The shopkeeper came out with three small chairs for the children to stand on to get an even better view once the parade started.

Annie warned us to stay by the shop front and not to enter into the passing parade, as it wasn't uncommon for children to be picked up and placed on the floats to be driven away, albeit in good fun. With their poor German language skills at that time though, no one wanted a panic attack from any of my three.

We stood waiting in the cold, but it wasn't long before the streets were heaving with locals and travelling visitors just like us, all awaiting the start of the procession. One lady asked where we came from as she could hear us discussing the events with Annie. She wondered whether we were on holiday, but Vanessa explained how we now lived in

Reutlingen and that today would be our first Fasching carnival, so we were all excited. The lady thought it fantastic that we had moved to her region of Germany, wished us all a happy stay and hoped we enjoyed the Fasching parade today.

The first thing we heard of the parade were whistles, so the children all stood on their chairs and jostled around to try to get a better view as the parade came towards us. Within minutes the sound was deafening, and the crowds were all shouting and cheering as the noise grew louder and louder.

The first sight we had was of a group all dressed in what looked like long white gowns with vines of hops printed all over them. They also appeared to have lime green shells hanging over their heads and shoulders. Every one of them wore a hand-carved face mask that must have taken weeks to carve and paint, each one decorated with a different facial expression.

Each of these 'hop people' carried a large wooden staff with bells attached to the top. They were shaking the bells as they walked, and with there being so many of them, the noise was deafening as they approached. At times they would stop walking, raise their staffs, shake them hard, all in unison, before hitting them on the ground … boom! It sounded like a thousand tambourines ringing, followed by the loud booming and crash as the staffs struck the road.

All the hop people were chanting and singing as this carried on along the street. It was an amazing start and the children were loving it, especially as one or two of the hop people had tried to lure some children into the street with sweets and small offerings. One or two of the older children had accepted the invitation of the wagging finger to join the parade and were picked up as soon as they were close enough to be 'abducted'. They were carried on the hop people's shoulders for a few metres before being released or escaping to run back to their parents.

While all this was happening, the whistling was getting louder and the noise more deafening. We had sweets raining down on us, so Annie pulled out several plastic bags for the kids to collect their sweets in so they could take them home later.

There was no time to stop or breathe, as next up a whole tribe of witches arrived, wearing ankle-length red skirts, purple aprons, black or dark-grey jumpers and purple headdresses. They too had wonderfully carved ugly masks, each different and hand painted to the finest detail, warts and all. They looked truly gruesome. They danced through the village and past us, and once again the whistles were loud and the sweets were still raining down, the kids loving this great new adventure.

Next up were a tribe of witches in green cloaks and bright orange headdresses. Each of the witches was carrying a broomstick, chanting loudly as they passed. Just as they came alongside us about a dozen of them threw their brooms to the ground and, in an instant, they had built a human pyramid, four witches high, and were waving to the crowds surrounding them. The witch at the top was throwing sweets to the crowds below.

As quickly as the pyramid had appeared, it was gone, and the scenes were getting more surreal by the minute as the procession carried on. Close by us, the children had almost filled their plastic bags full with sweets already, yet the parade was only ten minutes in.

Next up were straw men, covered head to toe in 6 to 10 centimetres of thick grass and hedgerow. Each held a twisted wooden staff and they went thrashing through the streets with a rhythmic stomping of feet and staffs on the road. Their faces were covered with the most realistic carved wooden masks, with beards and moustaches, and each wore pristine white gloves. As they passed by, they carried on pounding the streets, singing and chanting, then began throwing sweets to the crowds.

We were completely amazed at the costumes and were all participating in the joy and hype of the parade. There was so much cheering as each village float came past; however, this couldn't go on for ever and we could see there were only a few more to come through.

After some huge monkeys with thickets of brown, grey, black and red fur, who were all hopping and skipping around like overgrown gorillas and causing chaos as they tried to pick out the children next to the street, came tall, multi-coloured rag-and-bone people, covered from head to toe in small strips of brightly coloured cloth. In a rhythmic dance they swung to the left then to the right, then all dived to the floor on one knee before jumping as high as they could.

Just as this was happening, one of the rag-and-bone people appeared from the crowd and was enticing the children to follow for some chocolate treats. Before we realised what was happening, both Sam and Jake were off chasing them. They were soon in the middle of the street dancing and being lifted round and round the street by the rag-and-bone tribe. They were loving it, but it was a little stressful for me, as I was shouting away at the tribesmen in English to please let the children go. But they were in no danger and they were enjoying every minute, and after what could have only been twenty seconds, they were being led by the hand back to me, their nervous wreck of a father. And yes, they both had a huge bag of chocolate goodies to add to the rest of the sweet shop they had collected that day.

The last tribe through were also multi-coloured, wearing a black uniform with flashes of bright colour all over. They wore large, pointed, coloured hats, with black feathers in a large spray at the top. These were the first we had seen not to have a carved face mask but were wearing a full balaclava hat with a large white beard, red nose and mouth, and red circles to the eyes. Their hats carried on past their shoulders and had multi-coloured tassels all around the leading edge. Where did they think up these outfits?

I have to say this was the best village fete and parade I had ever seen. All the children had such a wild time experiencing their first-ever Fasching, and I reckon there must have been thirty to thirty-five different tribes, all masked and clothed in the weirdest of costumes. I knew this was one annual celebration we would be visiting again and again to participate in the fun, and for the children to collect a month's supply of sweets!

However, it was all over too soon and the crowds started to head off to find their cars. In true German style some celebrated in the beer tents that were also in abundance, for what would be another Fasching night to remember for the village of Engstingen. We, however, had to get home. The children were having lots of fun acting out the dances and chanting of the tribes they had seen, and also munching away on their bags of sweets.

We went back to Engstingen the following week, but second time around the display wasn't as enthralling as seeing it that first time. However, if you're ever able to visit one of these parades, please make sure you get there early, enjoy the atmosphere and take in this wonderful display of fairy tale characters that will entertain you like never before. I know it's a day we still talk of, and even though the boys were so young then, it has left such a lasting impact on all of us.

The hop people were the first of the procession to come past as the Fasching parade travelled through Engstingen

The gruesome witches in full glory as they travelled through, stopping for the odd photo opportunity

The rag-and-bone tribe came through and the twins went off on the hunt for chocolate

The weird-looking straw men singing and chanting through the streets and entertaining the crowds

Some of the many different tribes on display at the amazing
Fasching parade

Chapter 5

A Life Story Shared

LATE SPRING brought rain by the bucket load this year. It was lucky for us that the Germans in Willi's company didn't want to work in the rain, preferring to stay at home and wait for the sun to arrive.

No such luck for me, Steve and the other boys from the UK though. We were busy laying paving slabs and removing stones from some existing flat roof areas in readiness for the new roof coverings to come. All of this was being carried out over a three-week period during which it rained for what seemed like forever. And the biggest struggle was getting your clothes dry each evening for the following day.

Going into the second week of this wet weather, we were asked to install small granite stones and paving slabs to a large roof terrace in the centre of Reutlingen. The roof had no access for any kind for mechanical lifting machinery such as a crane due to the property being stepped deep into a steep bank. The access road to the house was too far away and too narrow for any form of crane to gain access or to lift the materials to the terrace. It was the kind of work that would keep you warm even when it was raining hard.

The size of the terrace was almost 200 square metres, and we had to move a delivery of 20 tons of small granite stones on to the terrace and spread them 10 centimetres deep to the whole area. Access was via ninety steep steps at the side of the property, around the back of the building and through a small garden, then through the access gate to the roof terrace, before distributing the material over the roof area. On each trip we had to fill our own bucket with stone, throw it up on to our shoulder, then off we would go, hiking up the steps, around the house, through the garden and on to the terrace. A round trip took about fifteen minutes.

Having got through the first morning, we took lunch in the works van, and for the first time the owner came out to ask whether we would like some fresh coffee. He initially spoke in German, but realising we spoke little of his language, he relished the fact he could speak English. However, it wasn't just any old English – it was laced with a mellow soft Scottish accent.

After an hour in the van, we reluctantly emerged to attack the pile of stones and get wet again. It took us two days to move the stones on to the roof. On the third day we awaited delivery of the paving stones, which we would again move by hand up on to the terrace.

Willi handed me a sketch of the terrace with a layout for the paving slabs and asked me to discuss the exact position of the paving area with the owner. When I visited the owner, he introduced himself as Lars and told me he was an avid table tennis player and the terrace and paving area was for his table tennis table. The slabs would provide a good area around the table for him to play without fear of stumbling on to the stones.

Having agreed the layout, we levelled the area, then once the slabs had arrived, we started to lay the paving, hauling the four hundred slabs over that same route.

After two days of laying the paving, Steve and the two other guys needed to go off site for a while to work elsewhere, so I was left on my own. By lunchtime I was soaking wet, extremely cold and my heart was starting to lose interest in the work. I had a gremlin telling me to pack up and go home to a warm bath, but then Lars arrived and invited me in to warm up. I think he must have heard my teeth chattering.

There was fresh coffee on the table as well as fresh rolls filled with hand-cut hams and cheeses. It was a meal fit for a wet cold king and I soon began to warm up. Meanwhile, Lars was enjoying his opportunity to speak English, something he didn't do very often. I had to ask where he got his Scottish accent from, as it completely disguised the fact that he was German. Even I could have believed he was Scottish if I hadn't known otherwise.

'It's a very long story Martin, but one I do love to tell,' he said, and with that he filled my coffee cup again and started to explain how he came to have a Scottish accent.

Born in the 1920s, Lars grew up an only child with his mother, in a poor family living on the Schwäbische Alb. He left schooling at thirteen and helped a local farmer with his cows to earn some money to help his mother cope with the hardship. Lars became a Hitler Youth member from the age of fourteen as it was a way to get additional food, which was extremely important in the mid-1930s. As part of this movement, he also received a uniform, and they provided him with some structure in his life. This was something that he had been missing throughout his younger years as his father had passed away before he was born. He explained how all those years later it was clear to him that the Youth was the start of what he called 'gehirngewaschen' … brainwashing.

Within the first five minutes of Lars starting his story I was mesmerised and couldn't believe what I was hearing. This man was in his seventies and was willing to tell me his life story just to explain his Scottish accent.

By the time he was eighteen, the war had been in progress for almost twelve months. It was now that he entered the Luftwaffe at the rank of Fahnenjunker (Flight Cadet) as he had studied aviation navigation with the Hitler Youth's aid and support. With schooling help and financial assistance, he dreamed of a great and proud career in the Luftwaffe.

After his initial six months of training, he was moved to the Dutch airfield of Bergen aan Zee, Alkmaar, in mid-June 1940, days after it had been taken over by the Luftwaffe. It was here that he started his short career as a navigator, during which he was guiding Fieseler Fi 156 Storch reconnaissance planes over the North Sea to take pictures and collate information from the UK to help his country's war planning.

By now I had been listening for over an hour to his tale and had just about forgotten about work. He went on to tell me that he recalled making only eight or nine flights. On a mission over northern England searching around the Sheffield area, his aircraft suffered engine failure. There was no option but to make an emergency landing and very quickly the three of them were picked up by the Home Guard.

After several days of moving from one prison to another, each time being questioned about their mission, the crew were separated. Lars was shipped to a camp in Scotland called Cultybraggan, in Perthshire, which was used to house German POWs.

His first six months weren't pleasant. He spoke no English at that time and none of the guards spoke German, with the exception of one or two Polish guards. It wasn't until he was detailed to a local farm from Monday to Friday as a farm worker, helping with the livestock, milking cows and working with a large herd of pigs that were bred for meat, that things got better and he started to learn English, albeit with a lovely Scottish accent.

Lars had a wonderful memory of his time on the farm, a job that he held for the next four years, with the exception that on occasion the camp needed him to help with construction works. He explained that when he started out at the farm, he had a grey square patch sewn on to the upper arm of his shirt or jacket, which meant he was a medium-to-high-risk prisoner.

As he put it, 'I was a shoot-to-kill prisoner, with no questions asked.' Eventually he was given a white patch, meaning he was fully trustworthy, able to carry out all chores given to him and was considered no risk at all. I asked whether by the time he got his white patch he was able to travel to and from the camp with no guard. 'Only on occasion,' he replied.

He would normally be delivered to the farm early in the morning, then collected each evening. However, once he was on the farm there were no guards and it just felt like home as time went by and he became one of the normal farm workers.

After eighteen months, Lars was considered so low-risk within the community that he was allowed to sleep at the farm to babysit. The farm foreman was happy to leave his children alone with him at night. It wasn't unheard of for him to be left a dram of the local whisky too, from the Edradour distillery. He explained that, to this day, it was still his favourite tipple. In fact, I had to turn down a glass when he started to open a bottle as he talked.

Although a German POW, he was by now treated just like a local. Many of the people from the village had sons fighting in the war, and Lars thought that they wanted to treat him and the other German prisoners the way they hoped their children would be treated if they were in the same situation. In fact, many was the time that the locals would completely forget that they were Germans.

Lars fondly remembered walking to the local train station occasionally to meet the latest delivery of POWs, to ensure they didn't get lost on their walk to the camp with their British escort guards. Not all the guards were nice though, and Lars spoke of the hatred the Polish guards had for all the POWs. At times this would erupt into punishment being given out by the Polish guards to settle scores, as well as to show who was in charge in the camp. Allegedly, a Polish guard shot one German soldier in the head for getting too close to the camp perimeter. Lars didn't witness any shooting, but news like that travelled very quickly in the camp.

Lars explained that he was also subjected to regular films that were shown to highlight the cruelties being committed at Nazi concentration camps across Europe, which had a solemn effect on him. He spoke of his sadness that regardless of the world being at war, we were all human beings, and that no one should have been treated the way the Nazi regime treated people.

It was clear that his time spent in Scotland had cleared his mind and body of the Nazi system. By 1943, he was courting a local girl, Kathy, who worked on the same farm. They shared walks and on occasion picnicked in the local area when he was allowed to venture out. He would spend all the free time he could with her, and although it was always a short time they spent together, it was a special time for them.

Kathy was his first love, and he explained that he still had fond memories of the time they spent together, how he still remembers her beautiful smile and could recall the time they spent working and sharing private time together for over two years that they were together on the farm. She obviously held a very special place in his heart from a time in his life when 'being German', in his words, 'was not a nice thing to be'.

Once the war was over it took over five months for Lars to be moved from the camp. He told me of his writing to inform Kathy of his release and return to Germany. He, like so many others at the camp, wanted to express thanks for the kindness shown to them, and to tell the world of the happiness and respect the local people had bestowed upon them.

Lars and Kathy had dreams of a great reunion once life had settled down in the post-war era, but alas he wrote to her several times over the first nine months of his return to Germany with no reply. It was a heartache he suffered for several years.

He had no further contact with Kathy and he never saw her again. He told how at the age of twenty-six it had been harder for him to leave her in Scotland than it had been to suffer the pain he felt when being first interned in the POW camp.

'Mein herz weinte an diesem tag,' he said … 'My heart wept that day.'

That afternoon was quickly disappearing for me as I sat and listened to the story of Lars, who was of the same generation as my grandfather. I had never heard such a loving tale. To explain to me, a stranger, in such detail about his first love felt special and something I truly respected him for.

I eventually managed to carry on working but by now my mind wasn't on the job. I had so many thoughts going through my head of the hardship this man had suffered. For the first time I was able to see the views of a German POW, a story I'm sure was much the same for many thousands of POWs, regardless of their nationality or which side of the conflict they were on.

At home that night I spent some time explaining my day to Vanessa once the boys were in bed. She too felt for Lars and the suffering he'd had to endure.

Over the next few days, with the others back on site, the work was finished on the terrace. On the final day, which also happened to be a Friday, we were all done and our tools were packed away by early afternoon. Lars asked that we stay for a short while, as he had a surprise for the four of us. We sat down in his kitchen and he brought through five whisky glasses and poured into each a generous dram of Edradour ten-year-old malt, his favourite.

I hadn't told the others about the story of Lars and his Scottish accent, or of his POW status during the Second World War. I felt it inappropriate at the time. Lars, though, raised a glass and offered a toast:

'To the ones we have loved and the lands that we share.'

We all replied with a strong and decisive 'prost …'

Fieseler Fi 156 Storch reconnaissance plane like the one Lars flew in

Cultybraggan POW camp

A prisoner's drawing of life in POW confinement

Chapter 6

The Arrival of Orangey

WITH FASCHING now just a memory as we entered March, spring was showing signs of appearing. The snow we had suffered during our first two months in Germany had also now finally cleared. I was working full time with the added option of Saturday with my company or with Franz, my new best buddy, either at his house or for one of his apparently endless number of friends, who also seemed keen for me to become their friend. Between them, they found me several small or large jobs, just to keep me working.

One of those friends was the owner of a very large car sales showroom. This was a well-known Scandinavian brand, built to withstand anything, so I'll let you guess the make. Anyway, he had a large flat roof covering the workshop area of the building, and it had several roof windows, which provided natural light into the servicing area. All of these windows had been leaking for many months, if not years.

The owner, Uwe, was another great guy. He invited me via Franz to visit him one Saturday morning in early March. I was to inspect his roof and, if possible, find out why the roof was leaking around the windows.

I arrived at 9.30am the following Saturday, along with Franz, who had come with me to introduce me to Uwe. Uwe had a very hard chiselled face and looked as though he had seen too much sun over the years, as well as smoked too many cigarettes, with his leathery skin and wrinkles.

Our first job was to have a coffee, which was loaded with a large brandy. If you hadn't already realised, Franz loved his drink — any time of day, any day of the week. It was my job to keep him happy, so if that meant drinking with him and his friends so I could keep working weekends, then who was I to argue?

As we drank coffee, talking through the problems with the roof, I inspected the servicing area inside the building, after which I visited the roof to look over the problem. Diagnosis was easy, as the felt roof coverings were perished around the roof windows as well as in several other areas. I advised Uwe that we would at the minimum need to carry out repairs to these areas but that he should start to set aside money to renew the whole roof as soon as he could afford to have it done.

To my amazement, Uwe instructed me to do both. First, he wanted me to carry out immediate repairs to stop the water coming into the building. Once this was done, I could carry out a complete new roof installation to the section of the affected roof. We agreed a day rate price for me to carry out the work, although Uwe insisted that I worked only until 3pm, as that was when his showroom closed on a Saturday. As he lived on site and access to the roof was via his apartment next to the roof, he wanted me to finish when he closed up.

It was looking like a dream job: start at 8am, work to 3pm, and Uwe was happy that it was Saturdays only, not to mention that it would be payment by cash. I couldn't wait. During the following week, I managed to get the materials delivered for the repairs, which would take me two Saturdays to carry out.

When I arrived on the Saturday for my first day's work, it was coffee and brandy once again, and I even turned down a beer chaser that Uwe was having. He then introduced me to his wife, Katrina, who hadn't been at home the previous week when I visited. She was a lovely lady, slightly younger than Uwe, and very sweet. She insisted that at 10am I stop work to have breakfast and coffee with them.

This really was turning out to be an ideal job; I was spending more time socialising with the client than actually working and I was getting paid at the same time. In fact, I not only had breakfast but had lunch with them too. I had only managed to work four and a half hours all day, but both Uwe and Katrina seemed over the moon with my progress.

It actually took me three Saturdays to complete the repairs and ensure the water had stopped coming in. I had been thinking that the main roof covering job would be done during the summer months when the weather was a little better, but no, Uwe insisted I carry on now and install the complete new roof covering. So, I asked Steve to help me, as getting all the materials, then working a four-to-five-hour day, just on a Saturday, was going to take weeks on my own. Uwe was happy for me to have some help.

As we came into the second week of April, we had two more weekends to go before the new roof covering would be finished. It was at this time that Uwe took delivery of three second-hand vehicles, each of which was bright orange. Two were pickup trucks and the last was a very old VW nine-seater minibus. When he was selling new cars, Uwe sometimes took used vehicles as part exchange, which he would then sell, if possible, or take to a local car auction to get rid of them.

The two pickup trucks had both seen better days and had bumps and dents all over them. They looked as if they had worked well beyond their life and were in need of some TLC from their new owners. The nine-seater bus, though, was in very good condition, and I took a quick look over it after we finished up work, before heading home. Uwe jokingly told me that the bus could be part payment for the job and that I should take it for a drive to show Vanessa. So, before I knew it, I was driving the vehicle home to show my wife and family.

Arriving home, which was only a ten-minute drive, no one took much notice of the bus as I parked up outside the house. I knocked on the window and asked Vanessa to pop out, which she did, closely followed by the boys, and we looked over the bus. I explained that Uwe had told me it could be part payment for the work I was carrying out, although how much of my payment would be money and how much would be the bus I didn't know. As Vanessa and I both liked the bus, I agreed to take it back and have a word with Uwe about his offer.

It turned out that the bus was an ex-local authority vehicle, as were all vehicles painted the same bright orange colour, not just in Reutlingen, but over the whole of

Germany. Uwe explained that this bus hadn't been used on the roads as such but as a taxi to take local authority transport drivers to and from their main vehicle parking area in Esslingen, a town halfway between Reutlingen and Stuttgart. This was where the state of Baden Württemberg kept all local authority vehicles of the local region as well as for Stuttgart.

He insisted that I keep the bus for the weekend and that I took it back during the week when I wanted to. So, I parked my old BMW up, locked it and left the keys with Uwe just in case he needed to move it. I then took the orange bus home for a few days' trial.

That evening, Vanessa and I discussed what to do on the Sunday and agreed that we should go out on a trip to see how we both liked driving the bus. We settled on the magical Hohenzollern Castle, which had been built as the headquarters of the Prussian royal family and the princes of Hohenzollern. It was only a one-hour drive and would give the boys a chance to check out the new vehicle, especially as each of them now would have their own row of seating.

Come Sunday morning, we set off around 9am, hoping to get there before too many other visitors arrived. The twins chose the back row of the bus, one left, one right, with a gap between them large enough so they couldn't hit each other. Meanwhile, Lee, bless him, finally got some respite from his brothers and could sit on his own right behind his mum in the middle row of seating. The bus was great, and it was such a relief to not have to be shouting at the twins to go easy on Lee, who was usually their punchbag while sitting between them. They would take turns to torment him to his young limit, as they pushed and punched him to despair.

Hohenzollern Castle is on a hilltop on the mountain of Hohenzollern, sitting 855 metres above sea level. Parts of the original castle were built in the High Middle Ages and date back to 1061, but the existing structure dates back to the early 1800s. The castle dominates the skyline as you approach and it's a formidable sight. It's actually quite difficult to get your head around the complexity of how they constructed such a beautiful building in such a desolate place on top of a mountain.

The boys were shouting out that we were going to Disney, but Vanessa managed to calm them down with 'maybe next year'. She told them that today we were visiting the castle of the local king. Well, it worked anyway, as they seemed to believe her little white lie.

Having parked up, we started the steep walk up to the castle. Thankfully, it was early spring, but I imagine this could be quite a slog in high summer. Arriving at a large gatehouse named the Eagle Gate entrance, you could be fooled into thinking it really was Disneyland we were arriving at. The castle has several tall towers with circular domes pointing into the sky. Each of the towers are a different height, the tallest of which has small, long and thin yellow-and-black flags that were waving in the light breeze.

We paid our entrance fee and headed towards the large internal courtyard. We were all awestruck by the place, even though the boys thought the castle was inhabited by a real king, possibly aided by his troop of knights and magicians.

Let's face it, when you're that age anything is possible in the imagination.

Looking up at one of the domineering towers, you could be forgiven for thinking that maybe, just maybe, there was a princess who had been awaiting her rescue for years and was in need of a knight in shining armour. Yes, it really is a fairy tale building, and so beautiful.

Our visit started with a drink and cake for the boys, as we sat and planned our route. We then spent hours climbing steep spiral staircases, firstly to get the best view of Stuttgart from the tallest tower, the city being over 50 kilometres away.

The main hall was a wonder, with its beautiful domed ceilings, ornate gold leaf and decorative effects. The large candelabras made one imagine what it would be like in the evening. The walls had decorative wooden cladding that showed beautiful craftmanship and there were also some wonderful hand-decorated medieval designs and frescos. Some areas of the ceiling were a deep blue colour that gave the effect of the sky looking down over the hall, giving the impression that the room was bigger than it actually was.

As we left the main hall and made our way through, we viewed several portrait pictures of past residents and monarchy of the castle. This area was in need of some TLC, as the wall decoration looked to be crumbling away; however, it took nothing away from the overall beauty of the place.

By now the boys were starting to get a little bored and were suffering from a lack of fizzy drink and crisps. We hadn't seen any sort of play area or park either. Their interest in medieval castles was wearing thin but we managed to keep the enthusiasm going for another half an hour with a trip into the cellar regions of the castle. I gave the boys the official guided tour of the dungeons and told them how the naughty children years ago were locked up if they didn't eat their vegetables. You have to give me credit for trying, but it wasn't long before we were saying goodbye to the fairy tale castle.

It was early afternoon by the time we left the car park. It was Vanessa's turn to drive the bus to see how she got on with it, and whether she would be confident enough to drive such a large vehicle. She had prepared a packed lunch, so we headed towards Reutlingen, stopping off twenty minutes later at a roadside picnic area.

Lunch over, with the boys strapped in, we decided to drive towards Stuttgart and just enjoy the rest of the day out, taking in some of the beautiful scenery. We drove through Tübingen, Herrenberg, then towards the town of Böblingen, the home of the US Army's 7th Army in Europe. Picking up the main motorway, we drove through the town and region of Sindelfingen, a small southern German city that lies close to Stuttgart, the headquarters and home to a huge Mercedes-Benz assembly plant. This would be a place we would later visit to see the sheer size of the plant.

Finally, after driving through Stuttgart, we headed for home, where Vanessa and I had a chat about the bus and agreed we both loved it. Yes it was old, 1981 to be exact, but it hadn't done too many kilometres and it was in fantastic condition. Our biggest problem was how to buy it and with what. We had no savings, as we were still paying off our debt, and getting some sort of loan was also out of the question, so it appeared it was just a pipe dream.

I took the bus back to Uwe on the Monday evening after work, and he asked how we had got on with it and whether the children liked it. I told him it was a great vehicle, but we couldn't afford it. Uwe laughed at me and said that was no problem. He asked, with a very straight face, whether I would like to exchange the BMW for it. That was a real no-brainer of a question for me, and I immediately said yes.

Uwe offered to buy my BMW and I could carry out repairs to his property over the next twelve months. He would only pay 50 per cent of my normal daily charge and the rest would go towards paying off the bus. As the price of the bus was DM5,000 (about £1,700), I thought this was a great deal, so I didn't wait to ask Vanessa, I just shook Uwe's hand and the deal was done. I took the BMW home that night, as Uwe needed to register the bus in my name and speak to Franz, who looked after my insurance policies. Franz would then organise the new documentation for me.

By the time I went to work at Uwe's the following weekend the bus was ready. He had calculated that I needed to work another fourteen days to pay for it. When I worked this out, using my daily charge, that meant he had given me the huge sum of DM3,200 for the BMW, which I had only paid DM2,000 for. He really was doing me a great deal.

I arrived home, had the obligatory bottle of beer to celebrate finishing the day's work and completing the deal, then had the added bonus of discovering that Vanessa was over the moon with the situation. The boys were also chuffed, and they spent twenty minutes looking over the bus, trying out their new seats again.

This bus was to make life on the road a much easier time for Vanessa and me throughout our period here in Germany. It proved to be a deal that we would never forget, especially once this first job for Uwe was finished.

After I had finished paying him back the time I owed him, I never charged him again for any work I did, but instead suggested that he hold the money for the day I wanted to upgrade the bus.

Even now, over twenty-five years on, my three sons have such fond memories of that bus and the fun we had in it. It's not often that getting a new vehicle makes such a lasting impression on a family and leaves so many unforgettable memories, but Orangey did just that.

The magical fairy tale Hohenzollern Castle, dominating the local region

Orangey, our new transport

Chapter 7

Fireworks and the Stuttgart Lichterfest

IT WAS early June when Vanessa's parents informed us they were going to visit later in the month for a holiday. They were missing the boys, who had been a large part of their life prior to us moving to Germany. There were no such things as video calls back then, so it was a weekly phone call to talk with family, and the boys would at best have a two-minute chat with their nan and grandad.

Vanessa was also very excited as they were to be the first visitors staying with us at Behring Strasse, and we both wanted it to be a great visit. We also wanted to be able to justify why we had moved halfway across Europe to live in a country where we didn't speak the language, which also meant that the boys and Vanessa were no longer a full-time part of their lives.

A couple of days later, when I got home from work, Vanessa told me that while they were having coffee together that morning, Annie had suggested we visit the Stuttgart Festival of Lights, or Lichterfest as it's known locally.

Vanessa managed to find some information on the event in the Reutlingen tourist office the following day. The Lichterfest is an annual event that has a very long tradition going back over seventy years, when it was inaugurated as the Night of the Hundred Thousand Lights in 1939. After a break during the Second World War, which resulted in Stuttgart's reconstruction, the light show returned as a brilliant firework display.

Nowadays, over thirty thousand enthusiastic visitors of all ages and nations wander through the colourfully lit heritage-protected Höhenpark Killesberg. Dancing, music and several other entertainments take place throughout the park during the event, as well as it culminating in Stuttgart's largest fireworks display, atmospheric illuminations and elaborate light shows. It sounded like a great night out and by then Vanessa's parents would be with us.

Two weeks later Diane and Jock arrived. It was great to see them again, and the boys and Vanessa really loved that week they were with us. Diane and Jock had missed their grandchildren, and the boys had missed them too. Vanessa spent the first few days walking the boys to their schools with her parents, then going into the city to take a coffee or just have a walk around the large shopping areas. They either did a little shopping or generally relaxed, as she showed Diane and Jock around the place.

On the Friday evening we all walked into Reutlingen and the boys were treated to a McDonalds, a luxury that we, in fairness, couldn't really afford to give them. It was a great evening, with the boys munching away on their burgers and chips while we all sat and enjoyed a beer. Yes, a beer; only in Germany can you buy beer in any shop or restaurant you can think of. Even the baker and butcher sold beer, which seemed to be a very important part of every German's diet.

I was informed during my time in Germany that a good roofer is measured by the amount of beer he or she can drink, especially during the working day. There were many occasions when I arrived, along with my work colleagues, at a private house at 7.30am, only to be confronted by a crate of beer and a bottle of schnapps from the owners of the property. At 9am we would be given a hot breakfast and again the beer would flow. This would be the same at lunchtime, when hot food, beer and schnapps were provided.

By this time, unless you had managed your flow of alcohol well, you were very light-headed and in need of an afternoon snooze. Not if you were a German roofer though; they just ploughed on until 3pm when out came the beer again, all supplied free of charge by the hosts. If you think this is a bit of a tall story, I can assure you it isn't. It was a real eye-opener for me when I first started working in Germany, just how much alcohol they drank.

Anyhow, getting back to the family. After a great Friday evening and a wonderful treat for the boys, we all had a great night's sleep and woke ready for the main event of the weekend, the fireworks show. Annie had suggested that we should leave at approximately 2pm for the one-hour trip into Stuttgart. I would follow her in the bus, which obviously had room for Diane and Jock.

When we arrived, the place was already packed, mostly with families. Annie wished us a great evening, as she was going to meet up with some of her old school friends and their families, while we headed into the park for a great evening and a night to remember.

The park was in full party mode as we entered, and our first surprise was the sight of the Killesberg diesel locomotives meandering through the grounds. So, we decided that was to be our first port of call, then we could get orientated as to what else there was to see before the firework display later in the evening.

Within a few hundred metres of starting out on the train we came across a very long inflatable obstacle course called Mont Blanc. This was covered with kids jumping, climbing and sliding, as well as the obligatory shouting and screaming, as kids do on these things. It was to be the number-one thing to visit when the train journey was over.

We passed several face painting stalls where we could see kids being painted as Batman, tigers, lions, clowns, and even Snow White, Mickey Mouse and Goofy. Again, I could see the boys looked eager to get their faces painted. I just hoped they didn't want me to join in too.

Moving on, we next saw a magician, who was dressed in his long dark-blue cloak with huge silver stars all over it. He wore a large pointed wizard's hat and held a luminous yellow wand that looked bigger than him. At a guess it must have been nearly two metres long and the thickness of a banana. There were kids of all ages surrounding his small stage, with shrieks of laughter coming from them at the magic show that was being performed.

Next on the journey was a stall with what looked like large transparent balls that had multicoloured lights in them and were attached to thin wooden sticks. They were being handed out to children and their parents. We had no idea what they were but intended to find out later. Then we saw just what the boys would really like, a huge adventure playground, which we later found out was one of three in the park. They were so big that I would guess over five hundred children could play on the swings, merry-go-rounds, slides, seesaws and the many other pieces of apparatus in them.

It took us almost forty minutes to make a full circuit around the park. Once back, we decided to walk the same route, first heading to the bouncy castle world of Mont Blanc. After an hour's drive to get to the park and another forty minutes on the train, the boys needed to get rid of some energy, and Vanessa and I needed a bit of a rest too.

It was twenty minutes later before we managed to spot the boys, all playing on the inflatable mountain range. They were having a ball, jumping, and shouting at each other. It took the promise of an ice cream to get them off the thing. They were sweating so much that they had to strip off their T-shirts but, ice cream in hand, it was off to the face painting.

Jock was encouraging the boys to get themselves painted as teenage mutant ninja turtles, their favourite cartoon of the time, which was fine but they couldn't agree who was going to be who from Michelangelo, Donatello, Raphael and Leonardo. To be honest, the only difference would be the colour of the bandana that covered their eyes – either red, blue, orange or purple. By the time we got to the first face painting clown, Jock had it all sorted: Sam was to be Michelangelo with the orange bandana, Jake was Donatello with the purple bandana, and Lee chose to be the red bandana of Raphael. It took only ten minutes for the boys to be transformed, and how I wish I had a photo of the three mutant turtles from that day. They looked awesome, and they were also now in top fighting mode, with their karate kicks and waving arms. It was very hard work calming them down as we ventured on.

We then took a walk around the huge lake at the bottom of the park and found another magician show, which we hoped would calm the boys somewhat. The magician was great, and it was more of a comedy show than a magic show. I really don't think I actually saw any magic, not that the children hadn't already worked out how he was doing it anyway. But he did get an awful lot of laughter and shrieks as the children shouted and yelled, telling him what he was or wasn't doing right, and how he could rectify each trick that he carried out. If I'm honest, it really was a great show, and the guy was a real showman.

Following this, we took a closer look at the large transparent balls with the multicoloured lights that we had seen from the train journey, but the boys didn't really show too much interest, so we headed for the adventure playground. Here the boys had a great time and got rid of even more energy, while us grownups enjoyed a cold beer as we sat and watched them tearing around the rides, screaming and having fun like any ninja turtles would.

The time was now getting on for 7pm, so we headed off to find our patch of grass for the evening and sat and listened to some of the live bands as we had our picnic. It wasn't long before the boys were up and ready for another run around, while the rest of us sat and discussed the lovely day so far. We wondered how long the fireworks would go on for and hoped they would be worth the wait.

It seemed a long couple of hours as we waited for the fireworks to begin, during which time the PA system announced a thirty-minute call for the show to begin, then a fifteen-minute, and finally a five-minute call. We sat ready as dusk started to set in over Stuttgart, as Tchaikovsky's 1812 Overture played in the background. This was one of my father's favourites, which I can remember having to listen to on many a Sunday during my childhood.

As the sky grew darker, the firework display started, in sync with the music, depicting the cannon fire from the raging battle between the French and Russian armies. The fireworks started to ring out and were extremely well choreographed to explode along with the music. The whole display was magnificent, and that particular music is a real masterpiece to set fireworks to. When it seemed to have finished just five minutes later we were convinced that was the end. How wrong we were.

For the first time since we had arrived the boys were silent, obviously still absolutely amazed at the display of dancing fireworks they had just witnessed in the night sky. What followed were several more pieces of music, including the soundtrack to *Jaws*, and U2's 'Sunday Bloody Sunday', accompanied by fireworks that were so loud and filled the sky in such colour that at times you could be mistaken for thinking it was still daylight.

After forty minutes the fireworks stopped, and again we thought it was over and time to go, but no one else was moving or leaving. Then, very quietly, the main theme from *Encounters of the Third Kind* started to play. As the music increased in volume, and in keeping with its tempo, the fireworks were released, louder and brighter than ever. You could easily have believed that an alien ship was about to land in Stuttgart that night. As the soundtrack rose to a crescendo, the fireworks became larger and more colourful, with vibrant blues, reds and yellows, as well as the most striking whites erupting in showers of sparkling spray.

It was one of those nights I would never forget, and to share it with the family was absolutely fantastic. By 10.30pm the fireworks were over and the boys were rocking to the display they had just seen. Most of the crowd was starting to move off and so were we, in search of the car park.

By the time we eventually found the correct exit from the park, and then the right car park, it was well past 11.00pm and the boys were very tired and grouchy. Annie's car had already gone by the time we arrived at Orangey, so we all jumped into the bus and headed home. We were only ten minutes into the journey before all three of the boys were fast asleep. Having had a full-on day, with lots of energy expended on the great activities, as well as the climax of one of Europe's largest firework displays, it was no surprise.

The following day we all thanked Annie for such a great recommendation. It really had been a fantastic day, and we had really enjoyed the event. However, it was all too quickly forgotten, as it was time for Diane and Jock to head off home the following evening after their short stay with us. It was going to be a very sad and solemn time ahead after such a fun week with them there.

Stuttgart Lichterfest in all its glory

Chapter 8

Lucky to Be Alive

MOVING FROM spring into the early summer months of June and July, work had been really great. I was with several other British guys all working for the same company, and we were having a great time on site. We were even picking up some German from our local work colleagues, even if most of it was some of the worst expletives you could think of.

The temperature was great though, in the mid to high twenties centigrade, and it was the first summer I had experienced with settled weather every day, unlike what the British summers can throw at you. Evenings could be a little sticky as we came into July, but several times a week we would have huge thunderstorms and torrential downpours, helping to clear the air and make the nights a little more bearable.

We were counting down the time until the first week in August when our good friends Dave and Julie would be visiting us with their children, Paul and Jill. Our children had grown up together over recent years back in the UK, and they were to be the first of our friends to visit us.

If you have read my first book, *Señor Lard Arse & Fat Man*, you will know that Dave was my riding partner and motorcycle mentor on our journey around the Iberian coast of Portugal and Spain.

Their visit was timed to coincide with my company's summer closedown for the last week of July and the first two weeks of August. I had arranged to do some private work with Franz on one of his properties on the Alb, about forty minutes away, during the first week of the holidays, which would also give me some cash in pocket for the time to be spent with Dave and his family.

As the time of our visitors' arrival drew closer, we were all getting more excited by the day. Gernold was even starting to learn a few words of English so he could at least say hello and goodbye in English to Paul and Jill.

They arrived in Reutlingen just after 5pm in Dave's brand-new Ford Mondeo estate, having travelled via Belgium, where they had visited Dave's aunt and uncle. Compared to our old VW bus it was like having royalty pull up outside with such a new and lovely vehicle. The children were soon off to the local park, and Julie made her way inside with Vanessa for the standard cuppa, leaving me to set about emptying the car with Dave.

With the car unpacked, Dave and I popped over to the park to find the kids chasing footballs and making a huge racket, just as kids do after so long apart. It was clear they had picked up from where they left off six months previously – the best of friends. We left them to it and asked them to come back together in one hour. Jill, bless her, is two years older than Lee and Paul, so she was the new mother hen, in charge of the raucous lads as they made a racket that could be heard from our house.

It was time to have a beer with Dave and Julie as we chatted about their journey down, what life was like here in Germany, and how our families were getting on. It really was great to catch up with Dave and, like the kids, we also picked up where we last left off, winding each other up and later trying our hardest to be as stupid as we could with the children to ensure they all had a great time.

That first night, the children were really hyperactive, and it was way past 11pm before they settled down and went to sleep. We couldn't blame them, as it was such a great time for them catching up. We adults, though, weren't as well behaved. As soon as the children were settled down, we really should have followed, but I'm sure we have all been there. It was time for a little music, a few beers, open a new pack of cards and chat away into the night. We caught up on everything that we had been missing out on back home and told Dave and Julie just what life was like for us here.

The next day we all went shopping for groceries, although Dave and I were told to take the children to a small park nearby, so the girls wouldn't be hindered and could get around quicker without the rest of us getting in the way. There were three water cannons in the park and the boys were taking it in turns to fire water over each other, as well as anyone else that came close by. It was good fun, but by the time Vanessa and Julie turned up we were all completely wet through. So much for leaving the kids with the fathers.

Vanessa and Julie took the car keys from us and we were told to walk the children home, but not to rush, as they wanted to get the shopping put away and have a coffee without us causing chaos for the next hour. We took the hint, and headed to the local garage en route, where we picked up ice creams and sat and ate them in the warm morning sun. It was a slow walk back, spending another thirty minutes in our local park, and we were home by early afternoon.

That afternoon was like many we had during the holidays. We took the kitchen sink bowl, half filled it with water, then popped half a dozen apples into it. We then had a whale of a time apple bobbing on the rear balcony with the children.

It was during that first visit of Dave and family that we came up with one of the best games for everyone to play after dinner. It's so good that even today we still play it, as we have such fond memories of those early games played during those holidays.

The game is very simple: You start with a chocolate Dickmann's, which comprises a biscuit base with a large marshmallow, about two inches tall, on top. The whole thing is covered with chocolate. There's a picture at the end of this chapter, and UK readers will see that it looks like a big Tunnock's teacake. You place the Dickmann's on a plate in front of you, then put your hands behind your back and try to eat it all in one. Our rules forbid you to bite the biscuit base, so it's very hard to get the whole thing into your mouth in one go. It's a great bit of fun, especially for the children, as they were so young at the time. I'm sure our neighbours thought someone was dying, as the noise was so loud as we all became covered in chocolate and marshmallow as the game went on.

Later in the week we went all in and bought some supersize Dickmann's, which are more than twice the size. Now that really was a whole different ball game, and only Dave and I could manage to get them into our mouth. However, eating them was impossible without dropping half the thing all over the table and floor.

The first week of Dave and Julie's visit was great fun. We headed off to see some of the local sights, such as the Bad Urach Wasserfall (waterfalls), which was a lovely walk through the woods to a nature park area. Here you could walk alongside the small clear river, spotting fish swimming, then up the side of the falls, where you get wonderful views of the Baden Württemberg scenery, together with the forestation surrounding the falls.

On our way down we stood under the falls on a small ledge and could just about look through the water as it fell. Even the twins managed to stand still long enough for a family snap under the cascading waterfall above our heads.

Thursday and Friday of that first week were real fun days. We had hot sunny weather, with no breeze and definitely no chance of rain. So, it was time to hit the Reutlingen Freibad, which was always a busy place where the children went to have fun.

What's the Reutlingen Freibad? Back then it was a place with several well-maintained grassed areas and four swimming pools, all different. The main pool was an Olympic-sized one for all the hardcore swimmers to keep up their daily swimming training. Right next to that was a 10-metre-high diving pool, where throughout the day the PA system invited children and adults to be taught how to jump from the 3-metre, 5-metre and 10-metre diving boards. This on its own was great fun, as you could watch the macho guys heading up to the 10-metre board to impress their girlfriends. More often than not, though, they realised they were petrified of heights when they got to the top, then like a cowering child they made their way back down to terra firma.

Next to this was a huge wave pool, so large that we couldn't let the children go into this one alone because there were always so many people and the waves were so enormous that they would wipe the children out very easily. Even when we did go in together, we always had to make sure we were on the very edge of the wave pool so the children could still stand up. By the time the waves got to us through all those people ahead of us, they were more manageable, but still enough that the children could enjoy it.

Finally, there was the fun pool, which was less than a metre deep and had stainless steel mushrooms sitting randomly in it, with water cascading out of the top of them. Two small children's slides also ended in different areas of this pool, and you were always guaranteed the very best of fun with the children when you went in.

Vanessa and Julie camped down next to the fun pool, laying down our towels over the well-manicured grass, in the way the locals did, for the demarcation of our ground for the day. Dave and I were straight into the pool, throwing the kids about, trying all we could to try to tire them out before the day was out. It was our tactic so peace would come early for us in the evening.

It wasn't long before the PA was asking for people who wanted to jump off the 10-metre diving board at the diving pool. I was volunteered to go first and made my way over to the concrete staircase by the pool, our group's sacrificial offering. I joined the queue with all the other guys, who were in their Speedo swimming trunks, posing for their young ladies. Me, I was just hoping the queue would be stopped before I reached the staircase.

No such luck though. After a twenty-minute wait, I was moving up the staircase, then inching my way towards the edge of the diving board, wondering to myself what the hell I was doing up here. If you haven't done this, I can tell you that the pool, which is at least 20 square metres, looks so small from up there. I thought that even if I did manage to jump, I wouldn't hit the water, but would more likely hit the concrete around the pool.

The young female lifeguard who met me at the top had to explain the routine to me in English. She told me to walk slowly to the edge of the board, not to dive off, unless of course I was a trained diver, which of course I wasn't, but to just pull my legs up and then dive bomb, trying as hard as possible to keep my back straight and head up. Finally, she instructed me that just before I hit the water I should hold my nose. I was shaking by this time, but I could see my children below, eagerly looking for their very brave dad, the fearless guy who was about to jump and show everyone that he was a hero. How little they knew!

Finally, after what seemed like a lifetime, I jumped. I remembered to pull my knees up, but completely forgot about the straight back and to hold my nose. I hit the water off centre, with my chest slightly leaning forward, water rushing up my nose and was partially winded. A few seconds (but what felt like minutes) later I emerged to loud applause from the crowd gathered around the pool, and all the children were smiling and clapping my achievement.

I felt awful. My chest hurt like hell and I looked as if I had sunburn all over where the water had hit me so hard when I landed. Or should that be where I hit the water so hard! I had survived though, but I can tell you I've never done it since, and never will again. Strange that until now, over twenty-five years after the event, I've just realised I was the only brave person from our little band to do that 10-metre jump.

The kids really enjoyed spending the week together, and still today we speak fondly of those early years in Germany. We remember the fun that we had on those family holidays we shared with Dave, Julie and their children, including the freibad and the endless fun we experienced during those hot sunny summers.

The holiday went so quickly that first year, and all too soon Dave and Julie were packing their car on the eve of their departure. I kept the children amused with the last game of apple bobbing on the rear balcony. Once the packing was done and the children were in bed, us adults sat down to enjoy a last beer or two and a game of cards, doing the best we could to not show we were going to miss our friends so much once they had gone in the morning.

However, by now I was suffering with a really bad headache, although I managed to see the night out. It was once we got into bed that I realised I had a real problem. My head felt as if it was trying to explode and the pain really was unbearable. I woke Vanessa and explained that I didn't want to wake Dave and Julie, but I was going to call a taxi, as I needed to go to hospital.

Within half an hour I was quietly slipping out of the apartment into a taxi, making the short journey to the local hospital. By this time, I was struggling to see, as the lights of the oncoming traffic were causing great pain to my eyes. Upon arrival, I walked straight into the accident and emergency department, but from that time onwards the next few days were just a blur.

After several tests, I was given a lumber puncture and diagnosed with viral meningitis. My temperature was sky high and I can remember being in a hospital bed, but not much more until I woke one morning with Vanessa and her mum sitting by my side. Vanessa explained what I had been through and that I would need to be in hospital for at least another ten days, providing my recovery continued to go well.

Eventually, after nine days in hospital, I went home. I felt absolutely knackered, as if I had spent a week in the ring with Mike Tyson. I found out later that Dave and Julie had no idea that I had gone to hospital. They had crept out of the apartment, as we had agreed, in the early hours to head north to Belgium, once again staying with Dave's relations. It was only that same evening, when they rang Vanessa to let us know they had arrived, that they learned what had happened to me. True to form though, Dave offered to drive back to help, but by that time Vanessa had already arranged for her mother to fly out to help look after the kids.

Looking back, it was a tough few weeks. I had a lucky escape that night, although it meant I was signed off work by the doctors for three months of rest and recuperation. Mind you, I stayed home only another four days before going back to work. I still felt useless and weak but we needed the money, especially after the holidays and the time spent in hospital or recuperating at home.

Thankfully, though, we got through it, and now it's nothing more than a story from our past, but it's a story we don't speak of too often.

A Dickmann's – you should give our after-dinner game a try

Reutlingen Freibad, with the Olympic pool (top right), diving pool (bottom right), wave pool (bottom left), fun pool (top left)

The 10-metre jump of fear! I made it, but it was a once-only gig that I was never talked into again. Even Dave wasn't silly enough to follow me to the top.

Stainless steel mushrooms in the fun pool provided endless enjoyment for all the children trying to sit on the top

Chapter 9

You're Going East My Boy

I HAD been back at work only three weeks when my boss
called me into his office for a meeting. I thought he was
going to tell me to stay at home to recuperate as I was still
extremely weak; however, I couldn't have been more wrong,
as I sat and listened to what Willi had to say, and what was
now being put on the table for me.

During the summer months, Willi had invested in the
opening of a new office base in Dresden, over 700
kilometres away. He wanted me to be his supervising
foreman, as well as being in charge of all the labour
requirements for the new venture. Well, not so much in
charge of all labour, but to supply as much labour as was
needed to carry out the work that he hoped to win. In doing
so, he would grow his business in the old East Germany,
thus helping to rebuild his fatherland.

This came as a real shock to me. Not only had I been with
Willi now for two and a half years, but he had given me
personal assurances that when my family joined me in
Reutlingen, I would never have to work far away from them
again. This was something I really believed he meant at the
time, and I'd had no reason to doubt it until now. I made no
immediate promises to him, as I needed to speak to the

guys who were working for me and, more importantly, I needed to discuss this with Vanessa to get her view.

When I told her my news, she was as shell-shocked as me. This would be a huge move and another big change in our lives. She and the boys had initially followed me out here to Germany for a six-month period, after which we had planned to sit down and discuss whether we stayed or all returned to the UK. However, they had fallen in love with our new lifestyle here in Reutlingen – the culture, the opportunities for us as a family, and being able to raise the boys in a very safe environment. Staying here in Germany would provide opportunities for the boys as they grew up – opportunities that we both felt the UK at that time couldn't offer.

We also had to think of the debt we were still paying off, and we needed another three to five months of my existing wages to ensure we were debt free for the first time in almost three years.

There was no choice really. Reluctantly, we agreed that I would get through this change of employment until our debt was paid back, and only then could we reassess the situation, finally making plans for the future.

The guys from the UK who worked with me here were very keen on the idea of moving to Dresden. None of them had seen much of Germany, and the new company would be paying price work in Dresden too, providing the possibility for everyone to earn more money. Price work means the work you carry out comes with a set price, so the more you do, the more you earn on a daily or weekly basis. This is a great system providing the prices are set at a rate at which you can survive, and preferably so you can earn more than you would normally do. If not, you can end up working twice as long for less money than you had been originally earning.

So, the plan was to leave in three to four weeks' time for our first project in the centre of Dresden and that we would be there for approximately six weeks for this first project. My only stipulation to Willi was that I wanted to return home to Reutlingen every weekend, as I couldn't leave Vanessa on her own for so long, therefore I would also need a vehicle. Willi agreed, also offering to pay for all accommodation in Dresden for the first three months, as he knew we already had places we were paying for in Reutlingen.

The following week, Willi, Steve and I set off to Dresden to deliver a new lorry and mobile lift, which was for moving materials from ground to roof level. Willi was in his car, while Steve and I took the lorry. The weather was fine and Steve was quite excited to be going east to see some more of the country, as he hadn't been far out of Reutlingen since he had been working there.

After a six-hour trip we arrived at the office/industrial unit, which was still being constructed in parts. It wasn't located in the city of Dresden itself, but in the village of Kesselsdorf, which overlooks Dresden. After dropping off the vehicles, we set out to spend the night at a local hotel, which was also to be our accommodation while working here.

After breakfast the following morning, Willi took us into Dresden, where we took a look at our first project. The carpenters on site were busy constructing the roof that we would later be working on. After this we drove to two other projects that Willi was hopeful of winning, both very large projects, and both in the centre of the city.

After lunch we headed north from Dresden to the village of Koltzsche, where Willi was planning to form a partnership with a carpentry company and enter into a local project in the village for building over eighty new houses. New roofs would be released every week, meaning this project would provide us with full-time work very shortly.

It was clear that no matter which way I looked at what was happening here, this was no short-term plan for Willi. It had also not been a quick decision he had made to open the new office and company here; this had taken a lot of planning and investment, and he was totally committed to making it work. If only I could feel the same way. By the time I arrived back in Reutlingen it was after midnight, and I was tired and very wary of what the future held.

The next day I discussed the labour requirements of the current contracts with Willi. We agreed that I would use only the English guys who were already under my employment in Reutlingen, and that we would agree each month the level of labour force that I needed to take to Dresden. We also agreed that the existing guys working for me would be guaranteed work back in Reutlingen if the work dried up in Dresden.

It was 2am on the following Monday when we left for Dresden, enabling us to be on site for 7.30am. I did this journey for several weeks, returning home early each Friday afternoon, so that I would be home in time for dinner with Vanessa and the boys and to spend the weekend with them. However, it wasn't long before this situation started to wear a bit thin for both me and Vanessa, and I'm sure the boys were also missing the renewed family life that we had been enjoying.

Within the first month of starting work in Dresden, a new roofing master, Uwe, joined us as the company's face in the city. He was a really nice guy, young and very funny, spoke great English and was also very good at his job. His role was to discuss and agree with the clients when work would be ready to commence, ensure we had materials on site, and start to look for further work to build up the company.

Things moved very quickly, so by the time we reached November, only three months into this new company venture for Willi, I had nine men from the UK working full time. We were also working seven days a week, with me still travelling home every weekend.

One morning two or three weeks before Christmas, Willi called me into his office for a meeting to discuss a new project. He had landed a project in Annaberg-Buchholz, a town about 100 kilometres from Dresden, but closer to Reutlingen. It's an old winter ski resort and, as we found out, it's very cold, with just as much if not more snow during the winter than Reutlingen.

Our meeting that morning was to discuss the best slates to install on the project. Willi had three options from the architect and wanted my input into what would be the best slates for my British workforce to install. We looked at the project plans and I could see that it was huge, on a scale I couldn't imagine to be quite honest. I also found out that I would be going with Willi later in the week to view the project.

Three days later, we drove over an hour and half to Annaberg-Buchholz, which I thought was run down and very dreary and grey. To be fair, I suppose it was late November, so everything looked black and white, or grey, cold and bland. The proposed project was for over seven hundred apartments, a shopping centre and a sports centre, with parking for hundreds of cars. After Willi had dropped me back in Dresden, I sat trying to comprehend the sheer size of this new job. I realised that I was about to enter into my largest-ever job and this would mean committing to Willi even more labour than we had employed so far working in Dresden.

In Dresden, the weather was getting worse, winter was almost upon us, and over the next week or two leading up to Christmas we were regularly losing time due to snow and cold temperatures, which were down to minus eight. No matter how hard we tried, it was just too cold to work some days and we had to sit it out, earning no money, and most of our projects were now getting further behind schedule.

A week before we were due to shut down for the Christmas break, we attempted to start the Annaberg-Buchholz project, but there had also been snow there, and the roof area that had been completed for us to start on the previous Friday was now 30 centimetres deep in snow. Not a great start.

We had no choice but to abandon the project and make our way back to Dresden, where later that day I agreed with Willi that we needed to close the jobs down and call it a day for the Christmas break early. There really was no way we were going to carry out any work in that weather in the week ahead. However, by this time all the workforce, including myself, were suffering from the short weeks and small pay packets, so the festive season was about to be a tight one.

Christmas came and went, and in the new year we arrived back in Dresden to slightly better weather. It looked as if January was to be the month that we could finally start to get some money in the bank. With all the projects we had going on in Dresden, and the new project in Annaberg-Buchholz, I was asked to arrange for four new roofers to join us, which would help to get our projects back on track and hopefully to get some projects finished as soon as possible.

However, after two good weeks of work the snow was back, but this time four solid days of snow. I knew from winters in Reutlingen that this was game over for at least three to four weeks for us, and if it snowed again it would be even longer. Again, I had no choice but to discuss the situation with Willi, who agreed that I had to lay the new guys off and send them home to the UK – not their best start on the job. The rest of the workforce was given a choice of either going back to the UK until further notice or returning to Reutlingen with me, but that was no guarantee that we would be working, as Reutlingen had snow too. In the end, only Steve went back to Reutlingen with me that week; everyone else went home to the UK.

It was almost the end of February by the time we all returned to Dresden, and I had agreed with Vanessa that I would need to do two-week shifts for the next few months to make up for the shortfall in earnings and to catch up on the projects. It had been agreed with Willi and Uwe that everyone was now to work at Annaberg-Buchholz, as the site urgently needed some areas to be made waterproof.

The weather was now dry but still very cold, so we were working in temperatures as low as minus ten that first week and production levels were understandably poor. By the time we got to Friday of that week and looked at the work completed, we had probably only earned about one day's pay each, which for all of us was disappointing as well as heart-breaking.

The workforce was falling into a deep depression, everyone feeling very low. We had now been earning very little over the past three months due to the bad weather, and I could sense the tension in everyone at that time. I spoke to Willi about the situation on the phone but, for the first time, he seemed very distant, as if I was talking to him but he wasn't really engaging in the conversation. He gave short answers, with very little conversation between us.

The next day, Willi's right-hand man, Klaus, arrived from Reutlingen unannounced. He had driven up the night before, stayed in our hotel, and I met him over breakfast. The rest of the guys appeared quite cheerful that morning, laughing and joking together, but I had this strange feeling of being isolated from everyone.

Just like Willi when I had spoken to him the previous evening, Klaus wasn't his normal cheerful self. Then after breakfast he asked the guys to head off to the yard to see Uwe about the day's work and he would catch up with everyone later. I was to go with Klaus to the office in Dresden. From that moment on I had a bad feeling about what was to come. I knew nothing about what was happening, and my feeling of isolation was even greater now. Why was I being singled out for a one-to-one in the office with Klaus?

Arriving at the office, I found to my surprise that Willi was waiting for me. This morning was getting stranger by the minute. Willi began to explain that it was his understanding that the low morale of the workforce was due to my not paying the guys their full wages. I was totally gobsmacked and couldn't believe what I was hearing. How could I pay my guys their full wages when none of us were earning them because we were all on price work? As of that morning, Willi had only paid us for what we had carried out – that's the way the system works. I told him straight that he had set up the price work, not me.

We argued back and forth for some time, but I soon realised that Willi was making me his scapegoat for the low morale. He was suggesting that the lack of work being carried out on site was the fault of my leadership, as well as me not paying the guys for work that none of us had actually carried out. I began to sense that the rest of the workforce, my guys, were in on this too, and I couldn't help but be angry with the whole situation.

Within the hour it was made clear that I was to return to Reutlingen with Klaus that day, and we would decide how to proceed with my workforce and all the contracts later, back in Willi's Reutlingen office. So, I drove back to the hotel and packed my bags. By 10am Klaus and I were on our way to Reutlingen, so I had no time to discuss any of this with the workforce, not even Steve.

I arrived home late that afternoon, and by this time I knew that I had been singled out to go, for whatever reason. Willi had clearly decided he could carry out the work with one less person on the workforce. Vanessa was naturally worried about how we would survive. My German was still very poor, so how would I get another job locally and with the same potential that I had with Willi?

The next morning, I arrived at Willi's office, where he was waiting for me. We had what turned out to be a short and sweet meeting. I was out. Willi said he had discussed things with the workforce after my departure the day before, telling them that things would be better with them working directly for him and not for me. My workforce believed every tale he told them – that I was the devil in the camp and surplus to requirements. It was his firm and his decision, but in my eyes though, I had done nothing wrong.

His decision was clearly going to affect me and my family's life considerably. I was being cast out due to circumstances that really were beyond my control, and I had also left without all the money that was due to me. It was a straight cut and the door was closed. Willi also didn't pay a penny in severance.

I had accepted his offer to go east and help expand his business, but for reasons I couldn't understand, I had been removed. I had been sacked on the spot and cast aside for the so-called better of this company. I was now jobless in a foreign country and was virtually penniless. My family depended on me and I had no idea what the bloody hell I was going to do!

Chapter 10

It's a New Start

TO SAY I felt depressed the following morning is an understatement. Vanessa and I were both shell-shocked at the situation we were now in. After several months with little work, I was now out of a job, with five mouths to feed and not much money in the bank.

Once the children had gone off to school, Annie popped down for a chat and catch-up. She too couldn't believe the situation nor quite grasp that I hadn't actually been employed by Willi. Being self-employed in Germany isn't as common as it is in the construction industry in the UK. Basically, it meant that I had little to no employment rights.

However, as bad as everything seemed, she did do a good job of cheering us both up, informing us that unemployment was under 2 per cent at the time in Germany due to the falling of the wall in 1989. She also explained where I should go to look at the job offers available in my trade, and she set about scanning the local newspapers for opportunities for me.

Within an hour Annie had found three options in the local papers, but only one was a roofing job. She then made a call and got me an appointment at the local job centre for the following afternoon. She wouldn't be able to go with me, but the gentleman she spoke to at the job centre said that if I struggled to view available jobs on their computer system, one of their staff would be available to help me.

After discussing things with Vanessa, we decided that I should go to the job centre first to see what other jobs were available before I tried calling the numbers that Annie had found in the local adverts. My German was still very poor at the time and I wasn't confident that I could hold a job interview over the phone about any position.

So, on day two of my unemployed status, I walked across town to the job centre. I registered at reception, giving my name and appointment details. With a little broken German, and thankfully some great English from the lady dealing with my registration, I discovered that I could use their in-house computers for one hour each week to search for employment. She also gave me a ten-minute lesson on how to find what I was looking for, as everything was in German on their system, with no option to change the language. With my computer skills back then being even worse than my German, I sat down, took out a pen and paper and started searching through the jobs.

It was quite simple once I had been shown what to do. I could choose the locality within which I was looking for employment, as the system covered the whole of Baden Württemberg. I started in and around Reutlingen and discovered there were several potential opportunities for me. I noted them down and took all the contact details. I then started looking in the neighbouring locations, as in Reutlingen we were very close to the town of Tübingen and the city of Stuttgart.

I found a great opportunity in the small village of Pliezhausen, between Tübingen and Reutlingen. The reason it really interested me was that it was a flat roofing company that I knew was quite a large concern, as I had previously worked on the same contracts as them. I was also known to several of their workers and had been given the name of 'the crazy Englishman', apparently because they weren't used to someone working as hard as I did. The other big plus was that flat roofing to me was by no means as difficult as tiled or pitched roofing, even though I was a fully qualified tiled roofer. I felt that it would be easier for me to rely on my abilities as a flat roofer given my limited German language skills. I also thought that it would be quicker and easier to take on a flat roofing job to help get settled in with a new company.

With that decided, I took the plunge and called the reception of this company. I could just about manage to call and ask for a meeting about the schwarz decker (black roofer) job. I spoke to a receptionist and was asked to attend an appointment at 2pm the following day.

I felt relief and excitement, firstly because I had managed the first hurdle of speaking on the phone in German, secondly for getting an interview booked, and last of all that I had a day to work out how I was going to explain in German what I was, what I could do and my qualifications and abilities.

I arrived at my interview the next day with time to spare. The sun was shining and now that it was early March it was feeling very spring-like, in contrast to the cold wintry weather I had left in Dresden just a week earlier. I spoke with the receptionist and was ushered into a meeting room, which had a huge table that could sit at least twelve people.

I stood there waiting, nervously running over and over again what I wanted to say in German. Minutes later the door opened and in walked a well-dressed middle-aged man.

'Hi Martin, I hope you're well. It's great to meet you at last,' he said in perfect English. He introduced himself as Horst Schmitt. I apologised that I didn't know him, but he clearly knew me. He then explained that his secretary had told him the day before that I had called about the position. He knew straight away who I was because Willi was a close working partner of his company and a personal friend. Prior to my arrival that day he had already spoken with Willi for a reference. Horst didn't go into detail about what Willi had told him, but he told me the job was mine. The only proviso was that Willi had requested that I wasn't to work on any of his projects, as he felt there may be a conflict with some of my old work colleagues.

Horst explained that he didn't understand why Willi had let me go but he thought it was a huge opportunity for him. I had an extremely good reputation within the industry and region as an extremely hard-working expert in my field.

I was absolutely gobsmacked. This guy knew more about me than I did. I had started the day with no job and worried about how I was going to survive but now here I was a few hours later being offered the position with this company and not even having to explain myself or my abilities. And not only would I get a new job, but I was to be his new ganger. He was starting a new gang of roofers for me to lead. I would get a new seven-seater van on my first day of work, and my work would be on price work again. However, I would get a minimum wage that was almost as much as the normal salary I had been earning in my previous job with Willi.

If this job was half as good as it was being explained to me, I would be earning more than I had previously and the hours would be less. Importantly, if I was asked to work away from home I would also receive a further allowance for that, which was something I had never had before. It was just too good to be true.

We talked over several contracts that we had both worked on over recent years and Horst explained that my German must improve in the next twelve months, but he didn't see it as any form of deal breaker. He then asked me when I could start, so we shook hands and I asked to start the following Monday. Things were tight at home moneywise, but not that bad that I couldn't spend a day or two enjoying some fun with the boys and Vanessa before work started again.

Monday came and I felt a bit nervous about starting the new job, as this company employed over thirty-five roofers and here I was coming in at the top. I would be one of seven gangers and was half the age of most of the others.

As I entered the building, I was met by a guy called Uwe Krust, who would be my contact and main link with the management. He would organise my materials and labour and ensure I had enough work ahead of me and my team as time progressed.

I was then introduced to a huge guy from Croatia called Goran, who was 6ft 8in tall, but who turned out to be the most wonderful gentle giant of a man. He was twenty-one years old, and I found out later that he was a Croatian who had lived in what was the Bosnian area of Yugoslavia. He and his family had escaped the war to avoid persecution or potentially worse.

Goran would be my first gang member. The second was a German guy, Thomas, who was the same age as me, but he informed me he would only be with me for four weeks. He had taken a job with the company as their new sales man, so his time spent working with me would be to get to understand the materials and their installation process, prior to going into the market place to sell them. Thomas spoke really good English, and I could see already that this was going to be a great partnership. I had youth with me, and a translator, and both Goran and Thomas seemed willing to listen and learn alongside me.

With all the introductions done and my company induction complete, we were ready to head out for our first job together. It was a little after 10am and I had been given my first job sheet. The job was explained, I had a working description of the task, and had hand-drawn plans and details for the work we were to carry out. We went to the stores in my new van, collected our materials from the list that had been given to us, and by 11am were on the road. Thomas, as a local, was the navigator. The new team was up and running and we were about to start our new working careers together.

Chapter 11

An Offer I Couldn't Refuse

THREE WEEKS into the latest job and I was loving this new challenge. With my previous job I always had a cloud hanging over me to make sure we had enough work coming in for the workforce to earn decent money. I was disappointed that they turned on me in the end, but I've learned over the years not to be surprised about people or what they will do when money is involved. Believe me, I've seen much worse than what happened to me back in Dresden.

However, my new work colleagues were great. Thomas spoke very good English and Goran was already becoming a great friend. They both wanted to learn about felt and flat roofing quickly, and they would never turn down a long working day if it meant getting a bonus at the end of the month.

Family life was great too, with the boys doing really well in school and Vanessa much happier that I was now working locally and coming home again every day. There was no more staying away for weeks on end like before.

On one Friday evening, our neighbours Sabine and Johannes, as well as Sabine's father and mother, Franz and Elsbeth, popped around for a beer in the early evening. The boys were playing outside at the front of the house with

Gernold and Madeline, and we adults sat around our dining room table drinking beer and making small talk. Franz was as ever the life and soul of the party. He was a huge presence in any room, and never short of boisterous comments and he was always joking around.

Sabine was having to translate for us as Franz was asking several questions about my new job, and I wasn't able to fully understand what he was asking, even with Sabine's help. Then he started to tell me about a good friend of his, Gunter, who had his own roofing company but wasn't actually a roofer. He was a businessman who had stumbled into the industry several years back. It turned out that he had lost his best man recently to retirement, and now only had two workers left, so his options were very limited. These two guys weren't fully trained in either flat or tiled roofing.

Franz's story continued, in between several other conversations, for about an hour or so, at which time he made his excuses and bade us farewell. Everyone else was still with us, and we were having a lovely evening. The children had now come inside and were still enjoying playing together. Most of the time all I could hear was Lee asking, 'Was ist das?' (What is that?), which was the main sentence he used for the first twelve months we lived in Germany. However, he did learn to speak German so quickly with a lot of help from Gernold.

Franz had only been gone ten minutes when the doorbell rang again. I answered to find that Franz was back but this time accompanied by a quite plump, tall man with full beard and a bright red face. The man was arm in arm with a rather lovely middle-aged lady who had a beautiful smile. Franz introduced the man as Gunter, who he had been telling me about earlier, and his wife was Helga.

I invited them in, having no idea what had been planned for me that night. Gunter spoke little English but he did speak very clear German, as well as the local dialect, Schwäbisch. Franz started to discuss Gunter's company, which was about 80 kilometres away, in the village of Waldkirch, just outside the Black Forest city of Freiburg im Breisgau.

Gunter and Franz were like a double act, explaining Gunter's company, its employees, workload, etc., and by the time I was on my fourth beer and Vanessa was being fed another glass of wine, Gunter asked whether I was happy with my new job. I explained how it was a great opportunity for me, I worked with some really nice guys and there would be further opportunities to come as my German improved.

Franz and Gunter carried on with their double act, then Franz suddenly disappeared again, with no word of where he was going. Moments later he came back with a large bottle of Williams schnapps and a small wicker basket full of schnapps glasses. He set out the glasses on the table and poured the schnapps. We all participated in the first toast of the evening, which Franz, in his best English, offered to 'nice roof-making men' (I think he meant to good roofers).

Gunter persisted with the questions, now about my past, where I had been working and the projects I had completed while in Germany. For those who know me well, there's one thing I can talk about all night and that's my work. I suppose it's because I've always regarded myself as a born roofer –

it's what I do best. Gunter then explained that he was looking for a man just like me – young, well qualified and full of energy – to help his business; a man with a view to taking it over in the years to come when he decided to retire.

Only now did the penny drop about why Franz had been here all night and why he had gone to fetch Gunter – I was being set up for a new job. I know you had probably already worked this out for yourself, but my German was very poor at the time, and I had drunk several beers, as well as trying to be the perfect host, so I was a bit slow on the uptake.

The next thing I knew, I was being invited to visit Gunter's company offices, as he wanted to discuss what it would take for me to join him in his company and to be part of the company's future. By now, Vanessa was listening to the conversation and it seemed the only people in the room who didn't know what this evening was about were me and her. Maybe we'd had one too many drinks, but I looked at Vanessa and she gave me that nod of agreement. I asked Gunter when he would like me to visit the company.

'In the morning is no problem,' Gunter replied. It was all happening very quickly and, with that agreed, Franz poured another schnapps and we toasted our new friendship.

So, at 11am the following morning, nursing a slightly heavy head, I was driving Franz's car, following Gunter and Helga, on my way to view Gunter's company premises. On the way there Franz was still trying all he could in his broken English to big the company up, but when we arrived just over an hour later there was very little to see. Gunter had a small office, toilet and kitchen, all of which covered no more than the size of a double garage. Outside there was approximately half an acre of scrubland, which was almost entirely covered with small piles of odd tiles and leftover materials, probably dating back years. If I had been brought here to be impressed, my first impression of his company wasn't great at all.

Gunter invited me into the office, while Franz made his excuses and disappeared across the road into a small restaurant. Gunter's English really was better than I had given him credit for the night before. He explained again that he was in need of a young man who could see the potential he had and to help rebuild his company to what it was before his top man had retired. He explained that he was turning down so much work, be it flat or tiled roofing, as his two employees weren't really good enough to be left on their own to install any roof coverings. For several months they had been carrying out nothing but roof repairs and very small private jobs.

I could sense there was an offer coming so I said very little, just nodding and letting him carry on. I really didn't want to cut him off or put myself in a position where I was telling him my terms for taking on such a challenge. However, the wait wasn't long, as Gunter reached into the top of his office desk and pulled out two sheets of paper, laid them on the table and started to read through what he was offering me.

It was a complete package: family vehicle for me to travel to and from Reutlingen to his office daily; a 50 per cent increase in the basic wage I was getting from my existing job; and a quarterly and annual bonus based on profitability and increased turnover of the company. As he carried on it became difficult for me to not get excited; however, I did have the sense to ask for the offer to be left open so I could discuss things with Vanessa before I committed to a decision.

That wasn't what he wanted to hear, and I saw for the first time another side to him. He refused to leave it open for discussion, saying it was a great offer and he needed my answer. He didn't shout but he had moved from 'I'll be your best friend' mode to 'you will do as I say' mode. I stood my ground, saying I was sorry but this was the best I could do, given that things had progressed so quickly from the previous evening when we had first met.

Gunter wasn't happy but my mind was made up, so we headed over to the restaurant to meet Franz for a drink. I was drinking coffee but the others were on the beer and schnapps again.

Having arrived home late in the afternoon with the offer letter from Gunter, I popped upstairs and asked Annie to translate it for me. Everything was as he had explained, with nothing lost in translation except the fact he had forgotten to mention I would also get thirty-four days' paid holidays, plus bank holidays. So that meant, with Baden Württemberg having fourteen bank holidays a year, I was more or less being employed to work four days a week and would be getting one day off every week as paid holidays. Annie suggested that it was a great offer, and it was clear to me that I would be paid far more than any roofer of my age and experience.

I discussed Gunter's offer with Vanessa over the weekend, as he wanted an answer sooner rather than later.

My only reservation was that I would be starting out from home at 5.30am and it would be past 6.30pm by the time I got home. However, by Monday we knew it was an offer not to be refused, so before I left for work I called Gunter to tell him I would accept and asked him to send the contract over. I told him that once I had received and signed the contract I would inform my current employer that I was leaving. Again, Gunter wasn't happy, as he wanted me to trust his word on the offer and just leave my job, but I wanted to have the security of the contract offer signed before I handed my notice in.

By Thursday of that week the contract was on the table. I signed both copies and took one to Franz so he could fax it to Gunter. I then went into work on the Friday ready to hand in my notice. It wasn't ideal, as Horst was a really nice guy who had taken me on without question based on my reputation and had made me a good offer. However, I had my money goggles on, and Gunter's offer really was too good to be turned down.

I tried to see Horst in his office first thing Friday morning. I had written my notice out in English but really wanted to tell him personally. He wasn't in at the time so I had to go to work, planning to try again later.

I went to his office again in the late afternoon and met him just as he was leaving the building. I asked if it was possible to have a few moments in private, but he insisted he was in a rush. I apologised, saying that I needed to discuss something with him that was important but he insisted that the fact he was running late was also important.

I had no option but to tell him while he was walking to his car. I handed him my letter. He wasn't best pleased, but he wasn't angry. He told me that if I wanted I could leave immediately if it helped my new employer, but the door would always be open for me. If the offer was too good to be true or if I didn't enjoy my new position, I just had to call him and he would reinstate me immediately. I thanked him and we shook hands.

When I called Gunter that evening, he was happy to hear that I could start on the following Monday. We arranged to meet on the Sunday afternoon at his office so I could collect my car and discuss the week ahead. Vanessa and the boys came with me, and it was somewhat of a shock to us that the family car I had been promised was a small Fiat van, with a fold-down row of seating behind the front seats. It had glass panels to the rear and looked more like a Noddy-mobile than a family car, but I realised that I hadn't actually asked what I would be getting; I had just accepted his offer. I had thought and dreamed it might be something nice. I learned a lesson that day, though, and it's one I've never forgotten.

We were only with Gunter for about twenty minutes, then we took a slow drive back home in time for the boys and me to head over to the park for an hour's fun before dinner.

On the Monday morning I headed to the address given to me for my first contract, and it was time for me to meet the new workforce. It was yet another shock. At the time, I had been working in Germany for almost three years, and I was used to being very smartly dressed in the traditional German roofer's uniform of black corduroy trousers, white shirt or polo shirt, black corduroy waistcoat and good-quality hiking books or shoes that supported the ankles. I wore a good-quality bomber jacket too and I could have gone anywhere in Germany and everyone would have known I was a roofer.

Gunter arrived first and we stood waiting for his workers, who arrived in a very old VW pickup truck, which was older than Orangey. As well as being quite badly beaten up, this vehicle wasn't a typical sight in Germany either, but when the two guys got out of the van I was gobsmacked. It looked as if Steptoe and Son had just arrived. One had a piece of string holding up his worn-out jeans, which were also full of holes to the knees. The second guy was wearing a 1980s-style shell suit that looked three sizes too big. Both were wearing trainers, and very old worn-out ones at that. It was hardly the forming of the 'A team' that morning, but there wasn't really much else I could say but good morning and let's get on with it.

Gunter introduced string belt man as Miri, who was a Bulgarian who had worked with him for over eight years. Shell suit man was called Slov, Miri's brother-in-law, also from Bulgaria, but he had only been with Gunter for a little over twelve months. Introductions made, it was clear that Miri, who spoke German at about the same level as me, was the top man on the firm, while Slov was his labourer and spoke no German at all. Well, if he did, he wasn't speaking it to me.

Gunter headed off and we set about our first day's work. It wasn't long before I realised that Miri thought I was a threat to him. I could sense that everything I did and asked, he wanted to do the opposite, and Slov just did what Miri said.

It really was a strange day and when I got home that night I felt really down and dejected about the whole situation. However, Vanessa did all she could to cheer me up and told me to stop being so negative. It was only natural that as another foreign national coming into the workforce as their proposed new boss, I would be seen as a threat.

Day two was no better though. During the morning, we all met on site then just got stuck into our work. Conversation was very limited and by lunchtime I was happy to get off the roof and sit in the Noddy car to eat. After that, though, I had no choice, as we were about to start on an area of the tiled roof covering that Miri had been working on during the morning, but I could see that he hadn't been installing the tiles correctly. Although I tried speaking with him about it, I was being ignored. So, I had no choice but to raise my voice and shout at him in both English and German, ordering him to stop and watch what I did to correct the area he had been working on.

Miri and Slov both stood and watched me for just over ten minutes until I had finished. I then explained that this was how this installation should always be carried out. Miri looked at me, nodded, then said, 'Okay Mr Martin, you tile roof boss, me flat roof boss.' I smiled and just carried on, but at least we were speaking.

I was right about both Miri and Slov thinking their position was under threat, but at least we were starting to talk now, and the week started getting better as they realised that I was far more qualified than they were on pitched roofing. By Wednesday afternoon they were actively seeking instruction, which made me feel much better. At least I didn't have to keep telling them to stop doing things wrong now, as they only did what I actually told them to do.

We worked for just over two weeks on that project, and although things did get a little better, the fun wasn't in the job. Miri and Slov didn't go the extra mile to welcome me, they just seemed to accept me, and each time Gunter arrived on site Miri made a beeline for him to show him what had been done and how well the roof was coming on. I really didn't have the energy to say anything to Gunter about the situation. I felt like an outsider and Gunter really didn't seem to want to help the situation. He didn't even inform them that I was supposed to be the ganger, the lead person here now. Yes, the new messiah of the company.

After the project was finished, we moved on to a small development where we were to install felt roof coverings to six balconies on a new construction. Miri immediately reminded me on the morning of the first day that he was the flat roof boss. Gunter came out to the job with us on the first morning, and even though I had been employed as the new roofing master or chargehand, it was Miri who received the instructions on what was to be carried out that day.

I could sense the pride in Miri's chest when Gunter departed, as he was left to then explain what was to happen to me and Slov. I bit my lip and just carried on. At mid-morning we stopped for coffee and a sandwich, and Miri asked me to follow him to the balcony he was working on, where he showed me the work he had carried out to a PVC door. I think he was trying to show and tell me that what he had done was correct and that I should carry out my work the same way. However, I stood in horror looking at the condition of the PVC door he had installed the felt to. The door was bright orange where he had overused his hot gas gun to heat the felt. He had burnt the door beyond repair. I told him he wasn't to do any more door works and that I would install all the felt works to the doors as I had a small gas torch specifically for PVC work. I would also try to clean up the mess he had made and improve its appearance.

How I wish I had just let him get on and do the job himself. Late afternoon, Gunter came out to see how we were getting on. I didn't actually speak with him; I just saw him arrive and leave ten minutes later. I didn't even know whether he had spoken to Miri or Slov either.

I didn't drive to Gunter's office that evening, but just drove straight home as the site was a good twenty minutes closer to my home than the office was. I did, however, pop to the office the following morning, as I needed to collect two gas bottles, and some gloves for protection. Gunter was there as I pulled into the yard. He popped his head out from the office and shouted for me to go in. As I entered his office he went absolutely crazy, ranting, raving and shouting about the PVC door that, in his words, I had broken by burning it with my gas torch. I was somewhat bemused at his behaviour to say the least and I asked where he had got the information from that I had carried out this work.

'Miri,' Gunter shouted. 'At least Miri can do the job correctly.' Now, with my mood and Gunter's attitude that morning, added to the fact that Miri had obviously told him it was me who had installed the waterproofing to the PVC door the day before, I was angry at his reaction and the aggression coming my way. I have a short fuse at the best of times, so when Gunter started getting aggressive with me, I did what I thought was the very best thing I could do on that morning: I walked out of his office, collected my belongings from the van, popped back into the office, took my office yard key and car key off my key ring, gave them to Gunter, thanked him for the opportunity and told him quite calmly to shove his job where the sun never shines.

Gunter looked at me, calmly asking how I thought I would get home from the office, telling me it was a crazy decision to walk out on the job after less than three weeks. I looked at him with little reaction or expression, and in a soft and controlled manner told him I had two legs that worked very well, and that he could forward my wages direct to my bank as well. With that I turned and walked out of his office.

I was so pleased with myself for not having lost my temper, but then it dawned on me that I was over 80 kilometres from home, had a rucksack on my back with my lunch and bottled water, and had a toolbox in my right hand that weighed over 20 kilos. This was going to be a long slog.

I walked for just over a mile before someone stopped and gave me a lift. They were going to Tübingen, near Reutlingen, so from there I caught the local train into Reutlingen and called Vanessa to collect me. She was, to say the least, confused as to why in the late morning I was at the train station and not at work, so I explained the day's events as we drove home.

I could see she was worried, as within the space of two months I'd had three jobs, the last of which I had just walked out of. I assured her we would be fine. I was sure that Horst would accept me back if I called or visited him. However,

Vanessa was distraught by the time we arrived home and was in floods of tears, so I knew I had to sort this out now. I immediately jumped into Orangey and drove to Horst's office, without any advance warning that I was going.

As I pulled up in Orangey, Horst was just walking out of the main doors of the building. He saw me straight away and asked how the new job was going. I quickly explained everything to him, apologised for my mistake in chasing the money with Gunter, then asked if the offer was still available to return to my old job.

Horst looked at me, a smile came over his face, and he said, 'Naturally Martin, we have a position for you. The deal is the same as before. You can start in the morning.' He then left me with his parting comment as he jumped into his car: 'Gunter is a hard man to work for Martin. I should know, he was my business partner for many years.'

Chapter 12

Back to the Day Job

IT WAS great to be back in a job where everyone was smiling when I turned up for work, even on a Monday morning. Thomas and Goran were still there, and it was business as usual when I returned. Thomas asked me whether I would be staying full time as he had turned the sales position down in the company to be part of the team I would be in charge of. I put his mind at rest and was glad the three of us would be starting out again together.

Vanessa was also happy that within twenty-four hours of walking out of a job I was back in the fold of my old company in Pliezhausen. We both hoped this was to be the start of enjoying the next few years to come.

It was now getting on towards the end of spring, the days were warm and summer was starting to herald its arrival. Dave, Julie and their children were booked to come out again for another holiday, and we had decided that we would drive into the German alps, to take a proper holiday together, walking and enjoying the mountains and fresh air.

I spoke with Thomas to find out about how to book a cheap bed and breakfast for the upcoming summer holiday. He advised that once we had decided which area we wanted to visit we should contact the local tourist board. We should ask them for a brochure of local accommodation, then go from there. It sounded easy but my German was still awful, so after further discussions with Thomas, he suggested it would be best to try a small region where accommodation would be better value. Also, if it was a walking holiday we wanted, it would cost nothing to walk and hike into the alps, as there are endless walking trails everywhere.

After researching our options, our first choice was Oberstaufen, which is about an hour and a half from Reutlingen and very close to the Bodensee, Europe's largest freshwater lake, as well as the German alpine regions. Austria and Switzerland are both right on the doorstep too. Thomas asked his wife to call the tourist board for me, as we were busy at work, and within the week a huge brochure arrived that included all sorts of accommodation in the local region.

Vanessa and I looked over the brochure for several days and, to be honest, there was very little we could afford on our limited budget. We did, however, look at several premises of the Deutscher Alpenverein, or German Alpine Club as it's called in English, none of which had prices quoted but were all price upon enquiry. They all looked a bit old, not run down exactly, but rustic is probably the best word to describe them. Each property had a German and English flag next to the advert to indicate that they spoke English as well as German.

I manned up and made the call to ask about the property that was our first choice. It looked like a huge property that slept over forty people, but from our understanding we needed to stay for a minimum of four nights and there had to be at least six people. There would be nine of us, so that was no problem. When I phoned, I reached an answerphone so left a message in English and hoped someone would call back.

Within an hour a lovely German lady who spoke great English called me back. I could tell straight away by her manner and enthusiasm that she loved the job she did, as well as dealing with people like me trying to find accommodation. Apparently, the property was a youth hostel, used by many youth clubs and organisations in Germany for school trips and outings. However, the good news was that they only used it during the school terms, not during the holiday season.

She informed us that the kitchen was communal and that we would have to take our own bedding and pillows, which was no problem. But the best part was the price – just DM7 for an adult per night and DM4 for the children. This was well within our budget so I asked her to hold the reservation for a day or two while I discussed it with the others.

Vanessa loved the look of the accommodation, and the map that came with the brochure showed several small mountain lifts into the region close by, as well as Immenstadt, a large town also nearby. After discussion with Dave and Julie, we decided to go for it and booked a six-night stay.

Meanwhile, I was settling into the new job. I was happy in my day-to-day work, the guys I worked with were great and I was getting home no later than 5.30pm every day. This gave me time to enjoy the late spring and early summer with the boys and their friends in the park across the road. Looking back at this time now, almost thirty years later, they were some of my most enjoyable family days. I had so much time with the boys and Vanessa, and it was just wonderful.

Vanessa and I were still learning German, but the boys were almost fluent after a year and a half. Having Annie living upstairs and Sabine next door meant that Vanessa was coming on great guns learning the language. I, however, had a different way of learning.

Thomas had become a close friend as well as work colleague and had decided it was time to stop speaking English now that I was living full time in Germany. So, over the coming years, Thomas spoke only German to me, even when explaining things. It was only one or two new words a day, and each week another two or three sentences. I was like Lee had been eighteen months earlier, asking, 'Thomas, was ist das?' but it wasn't long before I could hold my own. I was no longer totally relying on Thomas for everything, so when we had site visits by clients or management, or if I needed anything from the office, I started to ask for things myself with confidence.

******

Before we knew it the summer holidays were upon us. In my local region of Germany, businesses closed down every year for a four-week period in the middle of which Dave and his family were visiting. We also had our short holiday in the alps to look forward to while they were here, so it really was going to be a very exciting summer.

The weather was so hot that summer, with a constant thirty-five-degree heatwave during the holiday period. Most evenings we had thunderstorms, which were a real godsend to clear the air so at least we could get a decent night's sleep.

When Dave and his family arrived, we were back to playing games on the rear terrace, apple bobbing and hosing the kids down. The Dickmann's game was in full swing most evenings after dinner, so it wasn't just the kids who were having great fun playing games. Also, with the freibad open every day, this was a real cheap time, which is exactly what Vanessa and I had hoped for, as we needed all our cash for the holiday.

A few days after Dave and Julie's arrival, we spent an evening packing up all the food we needed for our self-catering holiday in the mountain hut. The kids were early to bed, having tired themselves out during the last few days with all the visits to the freibad, which was good news for us grownups. For the first time in a few days we could sit outside on the rear balcony, have a beer or two and relax without having to chase the children.

The following morning, we were all loaded into the vehicles and on the road by 8.30am. It was a great drive down, through hills and small villages, including Honau, from where it's a 200–300 metre vertical cliff winding up to the fairy tale castle, Schloss Lichtenstein. We had been up into the Alb region several times during our life here in Germany. It really is the most wonderful region, with the initial climb up the mountain cliff and then on to the flat regions of the Schwäbische Alb, said to be the foothills to the European Alps and just as beautiful.

We crossed the famous Danube river at Riedlingen, heading south to the larger town of Ravensburg, which was en route to our lunchtime stop at the lakeside town of Friedrichshafen, bordering the Lake of Constance, or the Bodensee as it's commonly called. Later in the week we would take a day out to explore this lake, with its almost seaside-looking towns on the lake edges. From here there are beautiful views of the German, Austrian and Swiss alpine regions, with their white snow-capped mountains.

After our lakeside lunch it was a leisurely drive, heading for our alpine retreat for the next six days just outside Oberstaufen. It was just after 3pm when we arrived, to be met by a lovely lady who gave us the key for our accommodation.

When I said rustic earlier, you need to try to imagine the scene that we arrived at. The place looked like a very old alpine cow shed. It was huge, consisting two floors, with the ground floor originally used for the cattle and the top floor for the family who farmed them. It had been converted into a very large communal kitchen on the ground floor, with a seating area that would sit over forty people on the traditional German timber tables and benches. It looked just like the festivals you see in Germany, where they're always laid out to sit, drink or eat.

To the other side of the ground floor there was an entertainment room that took up just over half the floor space of the whole building. There was a table tennis table, as well as a traditional German bowling alley, table football and an air hockey table. There were board games galore and an electronic dartboard. The kids were going to love this.

Upstairs was just as open plan. As you got to the top of the timber staircase there were two large dormitories to the left with twelve bunkbeds in each. To the right was a small corridor through the centre of the building with six small rooms, each housing a double bed and a set of bunkbeds. Three of these rooms had access to a small balcony that ran along the front of the building, all full of flowers, giving that real alpine feeling to the whole property.

The building was of timber construction and it was so old that the timber had turned a very dark brown. There was memorabilia everywhere from its farming heritage and some wonderful pictures of the building in winter and summer, as well as of the surrounding areas.

The lady explained that we could choose anywhere we wanted to sleep as we were the only people in the place this week. With that, the kids all headed back upstairs to find their chosen beds for the week, while the adults emptied the cars and brought in the cases and groceries, making sure the beer and wine went straight into one of the three fridges.

By now it was getting on for late afternoon, so we decided to get the kids fed, then they could run riot for the evening and the rest of us could try to relax, while planning the following day's outing.

Our first full day started quite early, as the kids were chasing one other through the dormitories and causing chaos by 6.30am. However, it was another four hours before we piled into Orangey, heading out for a trip where we would walk to the top of the mountain at Hündle. This is a small ski resort during the winter months, but the ski lift is still open during the summer for walkers and hikers.

When we arrived at the lift we were told to collect our free walking map in the restaurant at the top of the lift. Our only problem was getting up on the lift, which was a four-seater ride in the open air. We placed the twins either side of me, with them under strict orders to behave. Lee went with Dave and Paul, and Vanessa, Julie and Jill brought up the rear.

Getting off the lift was easier than we had envisaged, as there was a guy at the top to slow each seat down to let the children get off safely. Once on terra firma, we headed straight into the small restaurant for a drink and to pick up the walking maps.

If you have never visited the alpine regions during the summer months, it's hard to imagine that there are so many open areas to walk and explore. Mountains, whether large or small, appear to rise steeply and then decline with steep drops on the other side. How wrong that perception is.

The local region of Oberstaufen, although not at a great height, is entirely surrounded by mountains and meadows where cattle roam freely during the summer months. There are small mountain huts offering their own fresh fruit schnapps, homemade cheesecakes and fruit strudels, as well as the local high-carb spätzle pasta dishes famed in the Allgäu region of Germany.

After a quick chat and getting some advice from the lovely lady who served us coffee, we agreed on a quite easy walk through the meandering meadows of the high regions until we found the mountain trail to walk down towards the town of Oberstaufen. As we got close to the town, we could cut back on ourselves and head for our hostel. We were told it was a three-hour journey and that it was a very easy walk.

Once we arrived at the hostel, Dave would drive me back to the car park to collect Orangey.

A great first day was had too. Everything worked as planned, but we did take slightly longer to walk down, with the kids playing chase the whole way. The scenery was awesome, the air was fresh, the sky blue and not a cloud in sight. By the time we arrived back in the late afternoon the kids were shattered, and that evening they were quiet for once.

Day two was to be spent in the town of Oberstdorf, about a thirty-five-minute drive from our hostel. The town is dominated by the Nebelhorn mountain with a cable car that climbs into the glacier ski region high above the town, bordering with Austria. But we were here for something a little different. Oberstdorf is famed for its ski flying and jumping; yes, this is where Eddie 'the Eagle' Edwards displayed his skills back in the day. We were going to be visiting the Freibergsee, with its country walks and, if possible, visit the ski jump itself.

The lake sits over 900 metres above sea level and has the clearest water you could imagine. There are rowing boats for hire, a swimming area and a lovely restaurant that we would be treating ourselves to lunch in today. Added to this, there's a huge children's play area, not forgetting walks around the lake.

After lunch, we visited the ski jumping area, which had a very steep single-seater lift to take you to the top of the landing area. From there it was a short walk to the large concrete construction of the ski jump itself, then into another lift to the very top, where you could take a view down to the Freibergsee lake.

The view of the lake was just stunning, but the highlight for me was to take a look down the ski jump from the top platform to the landing area below. I couldn't believe how steep the track was that the ski jumpers travel down to build their speed prior to launching themselves into a jump. They can't actually see the area where they will be landing, so it's nothing more than a leap of faith as they launch into the air and travel almost vertically down the mountain face to the landing area filled with the crowds of high-adrenaline spectators below.

To take part in this sport you need to be absolutely fearless, with a high threshold for such an adrenaline sport. I know I wouldn't be able to do it but I fully respect all those, including Eddie the Eagle, who perform such daredevil sporting feats.

Unfortunately, it was over too quickly today, but we were really seeing Germany at its best, experiencing a culture we had never seen before in the UK. However, the next day was going to be one to chill out with a visit to the local freibad in the larger town of Immenstadt.

After a leisurely morning we headed out by 12.30 to the freibad, arriving just after two in the afternoon. This was nothing like the scale of the Reutlingen Freibad, but it did have inside and outside swimming pools, and large grassed areas to set out your towels and just sit and enjoy the fact that the kids could run wild and enjoy the afternoon in the water.

The week was shooting by, and the weather was just perfect. We packed the kids off to bed early after a barbecue as it was to be an early start in the morning to head back towards the Bodensee, in search of some more fun for all.

The following morning, we all jumped into Orangey for the fifty-minute drive to Lindau, right on the German border with Austria and on the banks of the Bodensee. It's an island town with two bridges linking it to the mainland, and it has boardwalks around the island and a small harbour from where you can take a ferry trip around the lake.

After a walk along the boardwalk and around the harbour area we headed back over the bridge for a walk around Lindau. Today was a more leisurely day and the kids were really well behaved too, probably feeling tired after three full-on days of activities. By early afternoon we headed back to Orangey and took a slow drive along the coastline of the lake. We had lunch in a layby next to the lake and just sat enjoying the scenery. We had a wonderful view of the Swiss Alps right in front of us, with their snow-capped peaks pointing high into the sky.

An hour later we arrived at the small village of Ludwigshafen, which is at the head of the lake. Here we stopped for a drink and some ice cream for the kids. We just sat on the banks of the lake in a restaurant bar, sharing this small area of the lakeside with many other families, their children playing in the water or in the playground and gardens. By four in the afternoon we were making our way back as the children were tired and it was to be an early night for everyone. Tomorrow was to be the biggest day of the whole week.

The next day we were away early, on the road for a surprise for the children. We were going to visit four countries in one day. Starting in Germany, we were heading into Austria for a fleeting visit, then heading south-west into Switzerland, then to Liechtenstein.

Once we were in Switzerland, we headed for the lake of Walensee, arriving in the village of Murg. We had travelled through some of the most stunning scenery during the morning, with the mountains rising to new heights as we reached Switzerland. Murg was a tiny village, much smaller than we had thought from the map we were using, but the views from there were absolutely out of this world, with huge steep mountains, white snow-topped hats, and lines of trees covering the lower levels.

By late morning we were back on the road and heading along the lakeside to the small country of Liechtenstein and its capital Vaduz. None of us had been here before and we weren't to be disappointed. It's a very strange country, where they speak German but use the same currency as the Swiss. Vaduz is only the size of a very small town, with approximately five thousand residents.

We had our work cut out today though, as there was a music festival taking place, so having parked up we couldn't really get access to any of the main areas of Vaduz, as it was ticket-only access. The only place we could get to was the main square, so we wandered around but there were only a few shops open because of the music festival.

The main attraction here was the Rolex shop, where only two people were allowed in at any one time. There were security guards on the main entrance door, and you had to walk in a clockwise direction around the shop. Only Dave and I went in, as it didn't interest the others, and we had a shop assistant each with us as we walked through the displays.

We were viewing watches that were on average in excess of $200,000. Yes, everything was priced in US Dollars or Japanese Yen. In the centre of the shop was a glass cabinet island with two more attendants. These cabinets held more watches, but the price tags on these were over $1,000,000. There were all sorts of precious stones in a lot of the watches, most of which I couldn't imagine anyone really wanting to buy as they looked so gaudy, but I'm sure they must sell.

It wasn't long before we were back outside and, sadly, it was time to move on, as there wasn't much we could explore in Vaduz. We checked the maps for a route back, but if you have ever visited the alpine regions and tried driving anywhere, you will be aware that once you leave the main motorways, driving is governed by using the valleys and mountain passes though the alpine valleys. So, although as the crow flies we were approximately 100 kilometres from Oberstaufen, our route back was going to be quite a long-winded journey.

Our trip back took us through Austria, some of the small winter skiing regions, then over the border into Germany, before arriving at our hostel just after 5pm. The kids were like constricted animals as they dived out of Orangey and started causing havoc once again in the garden. Who could blame them? What was supposed to be our best day of the holiday had turned into a bit of a damp squib, and the kids really hadn't enjoyed any part of the day.

Given this disappointment, our final day would have to be something good for the kids, as they needed to use up some energy. This would also help us adults to have a restful final evening before driving home the following day. After another barbeque in the garden, we decided to let the children choose between a visit to the freibad in Sonthofen, fifteen to twenty minutes away, or climbing a 50-metre-high waterfall close to Sonthofen, followed by a picnic in the mountains. It was a unanimous decision to go swimming at the freibad on our last day, so at least the kids would have a great finale and be knackered by the evening.

We arrived at the freibad by 10am the next morning. It had two pools, a 25-metre one for the hard-core swimmers with eight lanes to swim up and down all day, or the slightly smaller children's pool, just over a metre deep. On one side of the pools was a soft sanded area where you could play beach volleyball, and on the opposite side was a children's play area and mini golf.

The kids were soon stripped off and Dave and I were given the job of looking after them, while the girls set about finding a lovely area to lay the towels and set out our spot for the day. We couldn't have asked for a better day – thirty degrees, clear blue skies, and lots of fun for the kids to have. We did water sports, lost a couple of golf balls on the crazy golf, then got covered in sand playing volleyball. We stayed until the very end of the day to take advantage of our final day of the holiday, leaving at just after 6pm in the last of the afternoon heat.

The kids were shattered, and by the time we arrived home they were all a little grumpy. After a shower and dinner, it was straight to bed for them, while we packed the two vehicles ready for our journey home. We then sat down to enjoy a cold beer in peace and quiet in the warmth of this lovely summer evening.

It had been a great week, and this would be the start of our love affair with the German and Austrian alpine regions that would change our lives forever. We had fallen in love with the vastness of these regions during our short stay, in particular the unpopulated walking trails, the mountains and their views. Regardless of whether we spoke English or tried to use our German, we were made welcome everywhere we went during that week. The Germanic people we met were a warm and open-armed people. The locals loved to welcome visitors to their own individual regions of paradise and enjoyed sharing the beauty that nature had given them right on their doorstep.

Unfortunately, it had been such a short holiday and we arrived in Reutlingen the following day by early afternoon. I think we all shared a small sense of loss at not staying longer, as it had been the most wonderful experience, not just for the adults but also for our children. They had experienced the wide open spaces and the sense of freedom that the mountain meadows bring, as well as the wonderful fresh air. We would be back – we didn't know it right then, but later in our lives we would be returning to those alpine regions to have a very new experience.

As Dave and his family left the following week, we got back into our normal routine of life. I had another week of holidays before my company returned to work after the summer shutdown, but it wasn't long before I was back to the early morning starts. However, I was still getting home early after my 5pm finish, then having great fun in the garden or local park with the boys and their friends.

This is a time of my life that I remember fondly. I think also that the boys' friends came knocking just as many times to ask for me to go out to play as they did to ask for the boys to go out. That was a great sign that we were now being accepted in the local community. We were adopting the Germanic lifestyle and culture in our newly adopted country. We were also enjoying every single minute of it.

The beautiful fairy tale castle of Schloss Lichtenstein

Our home for the holiday

Vaduz Castle dominating the skyline above the very small capital city of Liechtenstein

View of the Freibergsee lake with the ski jump in the distance

The Heini-Klopfer ski jump with the Freibergsee lake to the rear

View of the Swiss alps from above Murg

Chapter 13

Me and Franz on the Schwäbische Alb

WITH THE end of summer now in sight and the nights gradually starting to draw in, I was in a great routine at work. Thomas and Goran were proving to be a good team to work with. As a roofing team, we were very quickly becoming a well-oiled machine, and each month we were starting to pick up some very good bonus payments from the price work jobs we were on.

I had been back in the job for just over four months, and even though I'd had such a long summer holiday with the company shut-down period, I still had another nine days' leave to take before the Christmas shutdown, plus another four bank holidays to look forward to.

One evening, Franz came knocking at our door and asked whether I would like to take a look at one of his properties on the Alb, which needed some work carried out on it. We agreed to drive up and take a look on the following weekend and that he would come to collect me early on the Saturday morning.

On the day, Franz arrived just after 8.30am and threw me the keys to his Volvo 850 estate. Obviously when he said he would collect me, what he meant was that I would be his chauffeur for the day. We headed out but after only ten minutes he asked me to pull in at a caravan and motorhome sales company showroom. Here we stopped for Franz to have a coffee and brandy with his good friend Franz Fitz. Yes, I know it's a mouthful but I swear it's his real name. I've often wondered whether he ever had trouble at school with a name like that.

Franz Fitz was a lovely man, about 6ft 6in tall, but with the most calming voice. He was a slightly balding man with a bit of a stoop, which was probably due to his height. He was approaching his mid-sixties and semi-retired from his caravan and motorhome sales business, which he had built up over the previous thirty years. His daughter was now running the business with her husband. Franz was separated from his wife, so he now lived in a self-contained one-bed apartment at the top of one of his showroom buildings.

We stayed for about a half an hour, and Franz Fitz invited me to return in the next week or two to take a look at one of the buildings at the rear of his estate that needed some repairs. I agreed, and with that we left, heading in the direction of the Alb, taking us up the vertical cliff beneath Schloss Lichtenstein. This was the same route I had recently driven on the way to the alpine region for our holiday.

It was only another ten minutes before we stopped in the large village of Engstingen. Franz explained that this was the village he had grown up in. It was also where we had seen the Fasching festivals in our first winter here. The property we were visiting was the house Franz had grown up in, where his elder sister, Margaret, now lived. She was there alone, as her husband had died several years earlier.

Before that, we parked the car on the main road and took a walk into the village. Franz explained about his years growing up after the Second World War. I could only imagine what life must have been like during his childhood days living here.

The village appeared to be in two separate areas, with the original side to the west, where Franz had grown up, and the newer areas to the east. He took me right to the edge of the old village to show me the wonderful and colourful small building that was, in his youth, the water source for the village, the well called the Sauerbrunnen (natural mineral spring). It has a colourful roof that has light and dark green, yellow and brown ceramic tiles. Each side of the building has a basin with running water coming out of a brass tap.

I had no idea how old this well was but Franz was really pleased to show it to me and to explain how this had been a place of great fun during his childhood, especially water fights during the summer months. As we walked back to the car, I could sense that Franz was extremely proud to have been brought up here.

As we came around the corner to where the car was parked, Franz stopped to speak with an old lady who must have been no more than 4ft 10in tall. She had an extremely hunched back, and from her withered facial features and wrinkled complexion, looked as if she'd had a hard life. The skin on her hands looked as hard as mine, with calluses on all her fingers, just like mine, which had been caused by using my tools every day at work. I guessed she must be a hands-on person, most probably working on one of the local farms. However, I never found out as Franz said his goodbyes and we headed off towards his family house to meet his sister.

Margaret was a lovely lady who welcomed me into her home and sat us down in the kitchen area at a traditional German dining table. Along two sides of the table were beautiful hand-carved seating benches with backrests, as well as four ornamentally carved wooden chairs that had large heart shapes carved into the backrests.

She made fresh coffee and placed it on the table for us to help ourselves. Meanwhile, I could hear that the language had changed from German to the local dialect of Schwäbische, one that I would be speaking in the years to come, all mixed up with a touch of High German too. Franz was like a child in the company of his sister, and I could tell by his change of demeanour that he had a warmth and great love for her.

Margaret asked whether I would like fleisch kugel but I had no idea what it was. I understood the word 'fleisch' as being meat, but 'kugel' was a mystery to me. After a coffee and some small talk, as well as listening to Franz and his sister talking away for an hour, we were served with a large plate of homemade German burgers. They were small in size but huge in flavour and came with a large bowl of salad and another full of homemade spätzle. My first homemade fleisch kugel was one of those times you always remember where and when it happened.

I won't go into full detail about what they taste like, but I will say that whenever I'm back in Germany I always head to the butchers for this delicacy. Trust me, if you're ever in Germany and you want to try this delicacy, the best place to find them is the local butcher in the mornings between 9am and 10am. Just have a look through the warm food selection and I'm sure you will find them. Just try one – it's a burger like no other, I promise.

As for the spätzle, it's basically an egg noodle, and again I have no idea how it's made, as it changes from region to region as well as country to country. It's found throughout the southern Germany regions, Austria and Switzerland. If you have the chance to try it on your travels, you're in for an amazing treat, especially if it comes garnished with finely chopped fried bacon and onions as ours was today. This was my food heaven.

After lunch it was upstairs to hang out of various roof windows, then back down to walk around the building outside to identify the work that Franz wanted done. I made my notes, thinking that the new roof coverings were no problem, but it would mean me taking the rest of my holidays to get them carried out before the winter came. I would also need help to get this size of job done in such a short time, so would ask Thomas, who could use up his remaining holidays. However, I knew that Goran could only help out on weekends as he didn't have much holiday left.

When it came to doing the job, I was in for a real eye-opener. Each morning Thomas and I arrived at 7am, when we would be fed fresh warm laugenbrezel, a traditional German pretzel, with loads of butter. It's a proper German breakfast, and again a real must have if you have never tried it.

Margaret would have a local delicacy that she also made called zwiebelkuchen (onion cake). Now don't turn your nose up at this, because served warm it really is the best cake ever, with onions and small pieces of bacon sprinkled with the local strong farmers' cheese. Thomas's local bakery made zwiebelkuchen fresh every Thursday morning, so from that week onwards, when we could, we would pop into his local baker and pick up a slice or two on our way to work.

Lunch with Margaret consisted of fresh bread rolls filled with cold meats and cheeses, with salad and pickles on the side. The only thing Margaret couldn't understand was that we wouldn't accept beer when we worked. She placed beer on the table every day, regardless of whether it was at breakfast, lunch or in the afternoon when she offered us fresh cake at 3pm. I've already explained how roofers were rated based on how much they could drink, but I was determined that we weren't going to join that drinking club here, especially as we were working three storeys up.

Franz would arrive each day between 4pm and 5pm and, true to form, would have a beer or two, then come up to the roof and spend time admiring our work. He would tell us stories of his childhood, being brought up during and after the war years, and tales of the people that used to live in the village during his youth. He also told us of some of the crazy things he and his sister had got up to during their childhood.

Eventually, if we were lucky, we would leave by 7pm, and I would drive Franz's car as he would have had too much beer. So, I would take him home and, if possible, immediately make my escape for the short walk home. However, normally Franz would entice me in for one or two beers. I had to fight off the offers of schnapps, brandy or whisky in his study before I could escape and get home to Vanessa and the boys.

Over the coming years, this would become a normal occurrence when I collected my money from Franz on a Friday evening for any work carried out for him during the week. Rarely did I get in and out of his study with my payment in hand without having to share a beer or two, as well as at least one bottle of local schnapps. Vanessa used to write off the whole evening when I visited Franz, bidding me good night whenever I left to visit him on a Friday. She knew I wouldn't have the willpower to say no to him. Why are women always right?

Anyway, we finished Margaret's new roof covering on time, and on that final Saturday we sat down for lunch. Franz had been with us all morning to help clear away any debris into a skip, but more realistically to generally get in the way. Naturally, he had already had a beer or two before we had finished the final clear-up.

Franz had invited his family, including Margaret, along with mine, Thomas's and Goran's for a barbeque at his house in Reutlingen that evening. After finishing lunch with Margaret, we eventually got Franz home and popped into his house for just the one beer. Fortunately, on this occasion I had an excuse to escape early as I needed to help Vanessa get the kids ready for the barbeque.

By 6pm everyone was back with Franz and his wife Elsbeth, with food prepared by Margaret. It was the first time since meeting Margaret that I had seen her with a glass of wine in her hand. She was staying over with Franz that evening after the feast.

Our kids were enjoying the evening too, as Franz had a huge garden, at the bottom of which there was a large tree with a great tree house built by his son-in-law, my neighbour Johannes. The evening went on into the early hours, and although the children were trying to keep going, they began to drop like flies. Thankfully, Vanessa had her sensible head on, as yet again I was being led astray by Franz all evening … well that's my excuse. Yes, I had one or two drinks too many – some things just never change.

Picture of Engstingen Rathaus (town hall) in the early 1930s

Sauerbrunnen mineral water well in Engstingen

Chapter 14

Our Lovely Scouse Surprise

DURING THE late summer months of each year, Germany hosts over a thousand wine and beer festivals. Some are more famous than others, such as the Oktoberfest, which is a world-famous two-week event that sees over two million people served beer, wine and some local culinary dishes in the Bavarian capital of Munich. It's a wonderful time to get out to try a few new beers or wines, especially as many are free samples. It's also a fantastic starting place to really embrace the local cultures and traditions.

Reutlingen is no exception, as in early September the city holds its annual food and wine festival, an event that takes over the whole city for three days. Although not on the scale of the Oktoberfest, it sees scores of local merchants and vendors displaying their food and drink.

In the two years we had lived in the city, we hadn't found time to attend the festival, but it was something we planned as a must-do this year, especially as we would have Vanessa's mother, Diane, staying with us. She had arranged to visit for a week, as she wanted to see her grandchildren and daughter. Her stay coincided with the festival, so it would be a wonderful opportunity to explore it for the first time.

I collected Diane from the local Stuttgart airport on a Wednesday evening, but the boys were fast asleep by the time I got home with her, so after settling into her new surroundings and unpacking her case we all had a cold beer on the terrace on this warm summer evening. We had made no plans to show Diane around the area as I would be at work every day, but we had arranged to visit the festival over the coming weekend.

On the following Friday we walked into the city, finding the route much busier than normal, especially the number of children with their parents. We headed to the main high street first, taking in all the festival had to offer. The boys were excited at the prospect, as their friends from school had told them of the numerous sweet stalls, with the traditional German gingerbread, endless amounts of chocolate and many different sugar-coated nuts. We would soon discover that it was a child's idea of heaven.

The city's main shopping street had become a village in itself. There were wooden craft stalls draped with different brown gingerbread hearts, each one ornately hand decorated with an endearing message in icing. No two hearts were the same colour, giving the effect of looking through a kaleidoscope. We had no choice but to stop and buy the boys a little something to keep them occupied, which would enable us, at the very least, to walk through into the main festival arena that had been set up in the large market place further along the main street.

So, it was pick 'n' mix for the boys, dispensed by a really friendly German man, who had a long white beard, plus an extra-long moustache trained to look like a Catherine wheel. It must have taken him hours each day to get it to stand the way it did. His stall of handmade chocolates, boiled sweets and so many other goodies smelled of wonderful sweet goodness, inviting all children and adults to come in and taste the wares.

As we moved on, within a hundred yards the stalls were becoming local crafts and hobby stalls offering anything from painting by numbers, sewing and knitting, and hand-crafted wooden goods. Then there were the local toy shops with their goods on offer to draw the children in once again.

I stopped at one of the woodcraft stalls as I was intrigued by the number of different schnapps glass sets they offered. After several minutes of looking it was a coin toss between two items. One was a wooden frying pan with six schnapps glasses that sat in neatly routed holes. The pan had a bicycle bell on the handle, which the boys found very amusing. I could only assume that if you rang the bell it was a notification to come and get your drink.

The second option was a miniature park bench made from small offcuts of twigs and wood that looked as if they had been foraged. On its seating area were six small holes for the schnapps glasses and to the rear of the seat, hand engraved with a hot iron, was the phrase: 'Ess warm und trink kalt, dann wirst hundret jahre alt,' which translated means, 'Eat warm and drink cold, then you will be a hundred years old.' How could I argue with that? If it meant I would have to try a cool schnapps each day for the rest of my life then I would need the bench to keep reminding me of this new-found proverb. So, I purchased the bench and all these years later it still sits in my front room.

The noise was building as we headed further into the festival, where families and partygoers were everywhere, enjoying the evening. As we entered the main market place, which is approximately a hundred metres left and right, the place was absolutely heaving with revellers. There must have been about fifty wine booths, each decorated in traditional décor, not one the same as the other. Each was packed several people deep with guests trying to buy or refill their drinks as they enjoyed the party atmosphere.

It was obvious we wouldn't be stopping here for a drink with the boys, as there were too many people to even attempt to enjoy it. So, we decided to take a walk through the busy market place and see what the festival had to offer on the other side. Grabbing the boys' hands, we headed through the scrum of people. As we entered the centre of the market place it opened up into a tranquil, almost humane calmness.

Standing in the centre of this area was a cart, although its horses had been removed and were in a small timber pen. By the cart were several young ladies in traditional dirndl dresses, each holding a small stainless-steel pistol connected to a thin rubber tube that led to the most enormous wine barrel I had ever seen, which was sitting on the cart. It must have been 2 metres in circumference and 3 metres long.

To the right of the cart was a small stall with glass tumblers for sale that were advertising the Reutlingen wine festival. You needed to buy the tumbler, then the wine being dispensed by the ladies was free. This was the only real option we had seen to purchase a drink without having to queue for ages, so while Vanessa and Diane looked after the boys, I collected three glasses and proceeded to get them filled with white wine from the cart.

The others had found a seating area close by the horses where we sat and enjoyed the wine, while the boys ate more sweets and watched the horses. It only took ten minutes before the boys became restless so it was time to move off and see what was on the far side of the festival.

Heading out of the chaos of the market place, it seemed as if the air became much cooler, probably only because there was more room to breathe now. We were soon trying local beers from nearby towns and villages, and the clientele of these stalls seemed a little younger than the people revelling in the market place. However, the younger generation were celebrating into the night with no hint of trouble. How the British could learn a thing or two about how it's done!

As we continued along the main street, the aromas drifting through the night really were wonderful, and we knew we were heading towards the food stalls. The first establishment was a large lorry with its rear fitted out with a counter where customers were served roasted chicken, and there were lots of customers. I can't imagine how hot it must have been to work inside this heated kitchen.

Next up was the local bakery from close to our home in Behring Strasse. They had two small stainless-steel ovens sitting on a table at the rear of the stall, each with three shelves where they could place ten to twelve bretzels or laugenbrötchen, a lovely bread roll, deep brown in colour, with a thick glaze and rock salt sprinkled over it. These are cut into two while still warm and spread with thick salted butter. They're a local favourite and a delicacy of the southern counties of Germany. Each bakery has a slightly different recipe and way of presenting them.

We weren't hungry but thought it would be nice to pick up another drink if possible. As we headed past the cathedral, the wide street alongside had several stalls selling wine and beer on either side. There was a small tent erected to our right, where we were being beckoned by a young lady speaking in a soft German voice to please enter for a drink. We decided to enter and get the boys a drink too, as we had been out for two hours now and all they'd had was a bag of sweets, with nothing yet to wash them down.

As the waitress came over, she recognised we were speaking English and asked whether we would like a menu for the food or just a drink. The amazing thing was that she had the most wonderful Scouse accent, not something you heard every day in Reutlingen.

We ordered our drinks, and as the waitress returned with them, she noticed we were looking at our wine glasses purchased earlier in the evening. It was then she informed us that we didn't need to pay for the wine that Vanessa and Diane had ordered, but she would need to pour the wine she had brought over into our own glasses. As the boys polished off their sweets and drinks, we had a wonderful chat with the waitress and found out where and how she had got such a lovely Scouse accent.

She told us that she had studied English at Liverpool University for three years, then stayed on for a further year to complete her Masters. She had worked part-time in several small pubs and a local fish and chip shop. She spoke extremely good English and was proud of her accent, but could if needed lose the accent, something we all found amazing. One minute she would have a Liverpudlian accent, the next she would be speaking the Queen's English, with no hesitation whatsoever.

Time was now getting on, especially for the boys, but for many this night would be going on well into the early hours. We walked slowly home, and by 9.30pm the boys, who had been getting a bit grouchy, were tucked into bed and I sat enjoying a beer on the rear terrace with Diane and Vanessa, who were sipping cold white wine from their new tumblers. We could just make out the music in the background as the party carried on in full swing.

By 11pm it was time for bed, having enjoyed a busy evening. However, all three of us adults were back up and standing on the terrace by midnight, as fireworks lit the night sky, filling it with bright colours and loud bangs. Five minutes later, near silence prevailed once again, apart from the music still playing away in the distance. Somehow, the boys slept through all of this and heard nothing, but they vowed to stay up the following day until midnight to see the fireworks for themselves.

'Eat warm and drink cold, then you will be a hundred years old'

Beer and wine stalls along Reutlingen's high street

German sweet stall – a child's idea of heaven

Chapter 15

The Local Derby

AUTUMN was now in full swing and our summer holidays were a distant memory. We were back into the final push at work before the Christmas break and were working on a large bank building in the centre of Stuttgart, which was a large penthouse with a huge 300-square-metre terrace in need of new roof covering. We had been given just over four weeks to do the job and were going to need all that time. There were some huge concrete paving stones as well as two layers of 10-centimetre insulation to be removed and stored to one side, all before work could begin on the waterproofing.

We had to drive past the new Mercedes-Benz Arena, the home of VFB Stuttgart, every day. The stadium had opened only a year earlier after a huge refurbishment, partly funded by the city's largest employer, Daimler Benz, ready for the hosting of the 1993 World Athletics Championships. The football team had then taken up residence. It was around this time that all three of my boys were showing an interest in football, each having joined a Saturday football club with a local team, training and playing with other boys of the same age group.

Thomas was a staunch VFB Stuttgart fan and a keen footballer himself but had stopped playing a few years earlier after picking up a knee injury. Goran still played for a local Croatian team on Sundays, but his local team was also VFB, so he followed them now that he lived in Germany.

During our second week on the job at the bank, Thomas and Goran were talking about the forthcoming visit of the most famous team in Germany, for what I discovered was the biggest derby match of the footballing calendar in the country, VFB Stuttgart vs Bayern Munich. Bayern's team formed a large part of the German national squad and had some of the world's top players, such as Lothar Matthäus, Mehmet Scholl, Oliver Kahn and Christian Zeige. They had also recently signed ex-VFB player Jürgen Klinsmann, who had just spent a season at Tottenham Hotspur. Bayern were visiting Stuttgart at the end of November for a Monday night match – VFB from Baden Württemberg vs the mighty Bayern Munich from Bavaria.

Even the boys knew all about the upcoming match, and their friends were divided about who would be the victors. Regardless of living so close to Stuttgart, most of the youngsters were actually Bayern fans. Who could blame them? They had all the big superstar names in their team.

Coming back to the job, we were visited on the roof daily by the bank manager of the branch, and also each week the local area manager would visit for a catch-up on progress and help to sort out any problems arising. Thomas would help me with all the meetings if I couldn't understand what was being said, but my first meeting with the area manager, Joachim, was no problem. He was in his early thirties and, I soon found out, had spent three years at Canary Wharf working for his current employer, before returning to his position in Germany during the previous year, so his English was fantastic. Mind you, most Germans speak great English anyway. It's just the majority of us lazy English who refrain from learning other languages.

Anyway, it wasn't long before football came into the conversation as he had been a part-time supporter of Tottenham while in the UK, and his footballing hero was Jürgen Klinsmann. Klinsmann was born and grew up not too far from Stuttgart and he had started his footballing career there, but alas he was considered a turncoat now that he was world-famous and played for Bayern. The upcoming derby match was mentioned, and I asked Joachim whether he would be going. 'Absolutely,' he said. 'It's a match I never miss now I'm home.' He told me it was always a great day out.

The following week after discussing the job and ironing out a couple of issues during Joachim's visit, we again got on to the subject of football. Before he left, Joachim asked whether we would all like to see the derby match as he was in a position to offer two free tickets for each of us, courtesy of the bank. Unfortunately, as wonderful as that sounded, I had to decline as I had three Bayern-supporting boys, and to choose who could go would be impossible.

Goran wasn't able to accept the offer as he would be visiting his parents in the north of Germany that week, using the last of his holidays. He was gutted to say the least, as he really loved his football. Thomas, though, said that although he would love to take the tickets, he would prefer to see me take the whole family and if there was a spare ticket he would come with us. That was it – I thanked Thomas and we all shook hands on the deal with Joachim. Mind you, Goran had the hump at not being able to go, so for the rest of the day we did nothing but take the piss out of him for missing the match.

I didn't tell the boys straight away about the match. I first spoke to Vanessa and we decided it would be better to tell them on the day, as waiting almost two weeks would be like pulling teeth as the boys would be so hyper. It wasn't long, though, before the Monday came around. I went to work as usual before the boys got up, and the plan was for Vanessa to tell them when they arrived home from school in the early afternoon.

After work, I dropped Thomas and Goran off and was planning to pick up Thomas on our way to Stuttgart for the match. The boys were bouncing off the walls when I got home, each wearing their Bayern Munich shirts, as well as being wrapped up warm for what would be a cold winter evening in the stadium.

Just as we were heading out, Thomas called to let us know he couldn't make it as his wife, who was expecting their second child, was ill so he had decided to stay at home to look after their youngest while his wife was in bed.

So, it was just us off to the footy. When we arrived, the place was full of families making their way into the stadium, with not a hint of trouble among the rival fans. Inside the stadium, as we walked around the outer walkway, we passed all sorts of food and drink stalls selling huge German sausages in a roll, large bretzel, all kinds of beer, as well as glühwein, the German staple winter drink, with or without alcohol.

After picking up some drinks, as well as some bretzel to keep the boys occupied before kick-off, we entered the main stadium to find we were right behind one of the goals and in a designated family area. The noise was deafening and there were huge flags being waved all around the stadium on really long poles that looked as if they could snap at any minute. We were in the Stuttgart family area, but nearly all the children were wearing Bayern shirts, most with Klinsmann's name and 18 on the back.

To be honest, the match wasn't the huge treat of football we were hoping for, although the boys enjoyed every minute of it. Stuttgart scored in the first half against the run of play and their goal was scored at our end so we could celebrate with the Stuttgart fans. Then just before half-time we were all treated to a famous Oliver Kahn save when the Stuttgart forward and German international, Fredi Bobic, shot from just inside the Bayern penalty area. Kahn dived high up to his right and parried the ball, then as the ball and Kahn came down he kicked the ball over the crossbar all in the same movement. Even now, twenty-five years later, all three of my sons and I still remember that moment like it was only yesterday.

So, Stuttgart headed into the break 1-0 up, and the stadium was rocking during the interval, although the boys weren't happy that Bayern were losing. However, they were so excited to be there, as it was just awesome to see. The second half was a little better for Bayern, and they were putting lots of pressure on the Stuttgart goal. True to form they equalised with just over ten minutes left on the clock.

We had planned to leave before the match finished to miss the crowds but there was no way we were getting out of there early as the boys were hooked on the match. The tension was now on the Stuttgart faces as the clock ticked down, then the referee finally blew for full time. The boys were convinced that Bayern had been robbed, but Stuttgart had just drawn 1-1 with the team that would go on to win the title that year.

It had been a great night, one we all still remember so well, and another wonderful memory from those years in Germany. However, not long after this, the boys' local football club organised a trip to Munich to see Bayern play the league's bottom club SC Freiburg. We made the trip in Orangey and took Gernold, who was another mad Bayern fan. Once again, we had a fantastic day out, with Bayern winning comfortably, 4-0. Mind you, it was against very poor opposition.

The highlight of the day for me though, was being at the Olympic stadium in Munich, the one built for the 1972 Olympics. However, another highlight was on the football field when Klinsmann was substituted early in the second half. He lost his temper as he left the field, kicked out at an oversized advertisement for batteries, got his foot trapped in it and fell over, which turned out to be a great source of entertainment for the whole stadium.

Jürgen Klinsmann – 'sticking the boot in'

Chapter 16

The Winter Flow Market

I GUESS not too many of you will know what a flow market is – put simply it's a car boot sale. The winter flow market is held every year in southern Germany during the last two weeks of October and the first two weeks of November. It's a market where you can swap all your winter coats, shoes and boots, as well as get new skis, or maybe sell your old ones.

So, why am I telling you about this? Well it all began when working on Franz's house on the Alb. Goran was always talking about skiing and how good he had been as a younger man before he came to Germany. Thomas had been brought up on skiing as a child and Franz had tried to convince us that he was an extreme skier in his younger days.

Now, I think I'm not alone in thinking it might just have been the beer talking. Anyway, shortly after the party we had at Franz's house after finishing Margaret's roof, he delivered his old skis to me at my home. This was a pair of retro 1970 Rossignol carver skis, light blue in colour and with bindings that must have seen use back when Noah left his ark all those years ago. However, I couldn't disappoint him, so with enthusiasm I thanked him and wondered just what the hell I was going to do with them.

The following day at work I told Thomas all about my delivery from Franz, and he suggested a trip the following weekend to the winter flow market to find a pair of second-hand ski boots and some appropriate clothing for me. After a brief discussion on the likely cost, Thomas assured me it was a really cheap way of learning to ski. It would cost a fraction of the shop prices.

Being so close to Christmas I talked with Vanessa about getting the boys some skis as their main present. We had two small ski lifts only a ten-minute drive from home, so getting use out of the skis wouldn't be an issue, especially during the months when I would be sent home from work due to the weather and put on winter leave with 70 per cent wages paid. We agreed it was a great idea, but we would need to go to the markets without the boys, as we didn't want them to see what we were doing. Thankfully, Sabine from next door offered to look after the boys for the morning while we went to the first of the flow markets and had a good look around.

I say markets, plural, as this weekend there were three markets advertised in the local paper, two in Reutlingen and one in the village of Sondelfingen, a five-minute drive away. We headed for the closest market first, which was housed in the local supermarket's underground car park.

The market was huge, full of people trying to exchange or upgrade the previous year's children's skis or buy clothing or slightly larger-sized stuff as their children were a little older and bigger this year. There were also some local sports shops and some national brands there, such as Nordica and Blizzard.

First on our list was to look for some stuff for the boys, and we found several stalls with used skis but nothing that stood out. The Nordica stall, however, had a great children's offer: skis, poles, boots, salopettes and ski jackets, all for DM199. They were brand-new and it was an offer that no one else in the market could get close to.

The queues were quite long but we decided to join, as this was such a good offer. When our turn came we discovered that we would need to pay a deposit for the deal now, agree a date, then visit one of their local sports shops for the children to be fitted for their skis, boots, clothing, etc. After that, everything would be delivered within seven days to the shop for collection, at which time we would pay the outstanding amount. The system was smooth – you could say Germanic – in that it felt like a very well-oiled production line.

We took up the ski offer, which consisted of salopettes, jackets and boots, and made sure that all three boys had matching skis so there would be no arguments. We paid the deposit, having agreed to take the boys for the fitting in mid-December. We were trying to keep this a secret for as long as we possibly could, as it would be their main Christmas present.

From the same stall Vanessa and I bought ourselves some brand-new Nordica ski boots. Both pairs were rear-opening boots, which were all the fashion at that time. Mine were black with a thin red stripe down the side and Vanessa had a white pair with a light blue stripe. They were DM40 a pair, which worked out to around £12. Unfortunately, we couldn't find any skis for Vanessa there and, as with all women, when it came to the clothing, what was there was either not the right colour, size or style, or made her bum look big. I'm sure you understand!

We headed to the next market on the other side of town, but we had obviously visited the right market first, as here there was very little but very old stock. The market was less than half the size of the one we had just been to, so it wasn't long before we were on our way.

The Sondelfingen market was the smallest of the lot, but it did have a good selection of used skis on a large private stall. With little else there we had a chat with the guy at this stall, explaining that Vanessa was a beginner to skiing and we were looking for a pair of skis for her. He popped to the back of his van and pulled out a pair of used Völkl skis, which had been his daughter's old skis. Although used, they were in very good condition and if we wanted them they were DM35. He said he would also adapt the bindings to fit Vanessa's new boots, so it was a deal done. He even threw a set of poles in for her too.

Vanessa and I agreed that we wouldn't tell the boys we were going to buy skis for them. At their fitting, I would discreetly tell the person in the shop that we didn't want the boys to know they were getting the skis, and to let them think they were just trying them on. This worked well as we weren't taking the equipment home that day. We could still make it a surprise by me collecting the skis and clothing the following week. We could then wrap them up and, bingo, the boys would have a Christmas present they would never forget.

So, that's what happened. After trying on the skis that day the boys got so grumpy thinking they weren't actually getting them. Even the lady in the shop told them that all the skis and boots were too small for them and they would have to wait another year to get some. The wait was worth it though. When they opened their presents on Christmas day it was awesome. They opened the skis first and you could see the happiness all over their faces.

We went on that year to learn the basics of skiing on the Alb just as I had planned, but it was obvious that we would need proper lessons to master this new sport. Mind you, that would mean travelling to a real ski region, not just a small local lift.

Chapter 17

Unterjoch/Oberjoch

EVERY WINTER and summer Vanessa's parents, Diane and Jock, paid us a visit. When we had visited them in the UK over Christmas, we had discussed the possibility of us taking a skiing holiday together, one where we could take a few days of skiing lessons then have great fun in the snow with the boys. My in-laws hadn't skied before but they were keen to give it a go, especially when it meant they could have time with their grandchildren.

So, in early January I asked Thomas for advice on the different regions that would be good for full-on beginners, and he suggested the Bad Hindelang region in the Allgäu, Bavaria, which is close to where we had been on our summer holiday the year before with Dave and his family. I called the local tourist information centre and asked for a brochure to be sent out.

Several days later the brochure arrived and we set about looking at accommodation to sleep seven people. This wasn't an easy task, as the time we were looking at was during the Fasching week celebrations, a week when families traditionally take a skiing holiday. This being the children's school holiday time meant that everything was more expensive.

With this in mind we decided to make a shortlist of all the accommodation we thought we could afford then we would look at where each property was and take it from there. There was no chance we were going to get one apartment for all seven of us, as the prices were just too expensive, so we were looking at two apartments. That made the search a little easier but still the choice wasn't fantastic. When we looked at the map of our shortlisted options, we found that all of them were quite a distance from the skiing region of Unterjoch/Oberjoch.

Finally, we decided to call each place to see whether they had availability, and as luck would have it our very first choice, which was also the cheapest, had two right-sized apartments available. We would be a short drive away from the ski slopes and the lady explained that she could help to arrange skiing lessons and ski hire, as she would get a discount. After discussing the holiday that evening we agreed to book five nights so that we could afford the lessons for three days as well as ski hire for Vanessa's parents.

With the holiday booked, I was still working, but it wasn't long before the inevitable snow and ice arrived in Reutlingen. It was mid-January, which gave us a few weeks to practise, or more accurately to slip and slide, at the local ski lift at the foot of the Alb. Not that we learned too much about how to ski, but we did have great fun trying during the several visits we made to this very small region, with the added bonus that the boys absolutely loved skiing from the off.

Mid-February came around very quickly, and before we knew it Diane and Jock had arrived and we were packing Orangey with our food and luggage for our five-day skiing holiday. The boys were hyperactive the whole journey there, which wasn't helpful, as traffic getting into the skiing regions of southern Germany during the main season is chaotic, especially on Saturdays, which just happened to be the day we travelled. What was normally a two-hour journey took just over five hours.

Our first sight of the skiing region was as we drove past the foot of the slopes en route to our accommodation. After passing through the village of Oberjoch, we headed down a very steep and winding mountain pass, dropping several hundred metres into Bad Hindelang and easily found our accommodation.

First job was to empty the van, then speak with the landlady about our skiing lessons, not forgetting to pick up the skis and boots for Diane and Jock. It was a busy afternoon as we made our way to the ski hire shop, which was a short drive to a small hamlet. The shop was tiny, the size of a large double garage, with a small winter sports shop on the ground floor, and below that a cellar for all the ski hire equipment, storage and servicing.

The elderly man in the shop spoke no English, although it wasn't much of a problem. He reminded me of the film *Chitty Chitty Bang Bang*, and the character Benny Hill played as the old toymaker. His movements and his mannerisms were just the same, and it took all our self-control not to laugh at him. But with the skis, poles and boots now in place for everyone, we headed off for the ski school, which had an office right at the foot of the ski slopes, at the opposite end of the skiing region to our accommodation.

We headed back up the steep mountain road, past the skiing areas to our right, and into a large carpark. After parking up we headed to a small hut with a ski school sign where we found Antonio, the boss and owner. He had a dark suntanned face and metal-rimmed glasses with mirror-finished lenses, and you could be forgiven for thinking he was a US fighter pilot. I got the impression straight away that he was a bit of a lady's man, and very confident with it too.

After a short wait, Antonio introduced us to our teacher for the private lessons, a young lady of around eighteen years of age, Johanna. She was a local girl who, as she explained over the next few days, was 'born on skis'. She had unbelievable ability on them too and proved to be a wonderful instructor with all three generations of us for the next three days.

We arranged with Johanna to start our lessons the following morning at 10am, but for now we headed off for a walk through the local area of bars and restaurants, stopping for a glühwein while the boys played in the snow, trying to build the first of many snowmen that week.

The following morning the boys were up early, all very excited and eager to get going on their skis. I'm sure Diane and Jock were a little nervous, I know I was, regardless of the fact that I had been trying to ski several times prior to this holiday with the family on the Alb.

Before I knew it we were parked up and at the slopes trying to get everyone into their ski boots, ready to walk the short distance to the office and our first lesson with

Johanna. She welcomed us and we moved off several metres for a team huddle and an explanation of what we would be doing on our first day. As Diane and Jock spoke no German, we had arranged for an English-speaking instructor. Thankfully, Johanna spoke very good English, so her instructions were well understood by all.

The weather wasn't so accommodating though, and within an hour of starting our first lesson it was snowing so hard it looked like a thick fog around us. It wasn't going to stop the lessons though, but it did add something to our fun on our first day as we were all struggling to see in the snow storm. However, falling over was made much more comfortable when there was so much fresh snow to cushion the landing.

Yes, we spent most of the morning falling over. The boys were really enjoying the lesson, and Johanna had her own way of keeping them in focus and observant, as us oldies did our stuff at a much slower pace than them. Each time they were asked to carry out something, she reached into her pocket and gave them a small chocolate sweet, something that didn't happen to me throughout the whole three days.

By the end of the first day we had all learned how to snow plough and to turn left and right. The boys were extremely good, far better than us oldies, who were just hanging on for dear life at times, doing all we could to stay with the programme. It didn't help me that my two-metre Rossignol skis loved crossing over each time I moved, and Johanna thought I was brave trying to ski with such long skis.

But we all had fun during our first day's skiing, and I must say Diane and Jock, who were in their early fifties, had a great time. It was their first time on skis and they had really embraced the day.

Day two and the snow was falling once again, but Johanna promised the sun would be out by lunchtime. Today we would be going to the small slopes for the morning, as we had done the day before, then in the afternoon in the better conditions we would take our first journey on a lift and start to explore the slopes above. So, we practised our T-bar pull lift technique and how to get on and off during the morning, as well as our stopping and turning again.

We were all excited when the sun came out in the late morning, Now the whole region had a fresh covering of snow and the tree branches were weeping under the weight of it. This was our first real sight of what would become our love affair with winter sports as a family, as well as skiing holidays that would be our main holidays for years to come.

The afternoon was much more strenuous for all except the boys. It was as if someone had given them a pep talk for fifteen minutes on how to ski correctly and then sent them packing, as Johanna mothered us oldies on the nursery slopes. The boys, however, spent the afternoon going up on the lift, then racing themselves down to go over and over again. Occasionally, Johanna caught sight of them and called them over, then each would get a little chocolate treat from her.

We four oldies were in no position to keep up with them. When they finally arrived back with us, Johanna gave them a few basic pointers on what she wanted them to do while they waited once again for the oldie group. Off they went shouting and screaming as they headed down the slopes.

By 3.30pm our second lesson was over and we adults were tired. Our legs, knees and feet ached like never before. Mind you, the boys were still at it, up and down on the lifts and having the best time ever. However, by 5pm we were back at the apartments, where Vanessa and her mum organised dinner while Jock and I sorted the boys and got them changed, showered and into their pyjamas ready for bed. After dinner we played a couple of board games with the boys, then by 7pm they were in bed. Us oldies didn't last much longer and were in bed by 8.30pm, exhausted after two full-on days of learning to ski.

The sun was out bright and early on day three, as were the boys after a great night's sleep. Today was the day of silly hats. Jock loves a hat and he had bought three fun woolly hats for the boys – one that looked as if it had bright-red horns, one with lots of yellow horns and the other with what looked like multicoloured dreadlocks hanging down. The boys loved them and couldn't wait to hit the slopes for the final day's skiing lessons in their new hats. There were no rules on safety helmets back then.

We started the day back on the lift we had been using the day before. My calves hurt on the first journey up on the T-bar lift; in fact, all my muscles still ached to be honest. I'm sure all the other oldies felt just the same, but the boys were gone. Johanna had spoken to them first about what techniques she wanted them to concentrate on for the morning, then they were off, like old-hat skiers, leaving

Johanna to concentrate on getting the four of us adults up and down the slopes.

It was a little like taking a group of Bambis out for a walk in the morning. However, come lunchtime we had survived our final morning's lesson, and we could all move around the slopes and get on and off the lift okay, albeit slowly. Diane and Jock were feeling a little more tired than me and Vanessa, which was hardly surprising, as they were almost twenty-five years older. They had done well to get through these past three days, enjoying this time with the boys on their first skiing holiday. They made the decision to sit it out and relax in the winter sunshine for the afternoon.

For the rest of us, Johanna said we should head off to the next level to where we had been during the morning, and we would take our first seated lift. Heading off, we could see the boys were really so good on skis. It really is a young person's sport to learn, as at such a young age they have no fear of falling over or that they may have an accident.

We mastered the seated lift that afternoon, then took Johanna for a thank you drink in one of the local bars after the lesson had finished. She was then heading off to the ski school to see who she would be teaching for the rest of the week.

The last two days of our holiday were awesome. Diane and Jock still skied but could now take it a little easier, enjoying a break as they felt necessary, and not having to push themselves to keep up with me and Vanessa. Mind you, none of us had a hope of keeping up with the boys.

The sun stayed with us those last two days and it was me who had the job of trying to stay with the boys while they skied all over the region in search of speed, speed and even more speed. I, on the other hand, struggled to keep up with them once we left the beginner slopes that we had been on with Johanna.

The boys took great pleasure in taking me everywhere they could. They made sure I fell over into ditches full of snow and we trekked through small tree-lined trails where the snow-filled overhanging branches smashed into my body and face as I was three feet taller than them. They knew exactly what they were doing as well; basically I was their amusement on tap. One minute they were going as fast as they could, with me trying to stay with them, holding on to my poles and skis for dear life, then suddenly I would be flying through the air as they took me over what felt like a huge ski jump, legs and arms flying everywhere.

Thankfully, I broke no bones that week. Mind you, I was black and blue with bruises from all the falling over. The boys would just laugh at me, telling me to get up and come on. And like a fool I followed. I was their ski doll, to be used and abused as they deemed fit. But what a great time it was, and we all really enjoyed it. Hats off to Diane and Jock though, what a great holiday for them it was, learning to ski in their fifties.

View of Unterjoch/Oberjoch

Me and the boys on the slopes

Chapter 18

Becoming 'Mein Meister'

WINTER WAS starting to move into spring, the weather was finally warming up and we'd had one hell of a winter learning how to ski. After our holiday, we had even managed to get two Saturdays skiing again in Unterjoch/Oberjoch. We drove down early morning to hit the slopes by 8.30am and took Gernold both times too.

I was now in need of some additional work over the coming weekends to start to build up the bank balance after three months of being on short time and reduced wages. So, I popped to see Franz on the Friday evening of my first full week back at work to ask whether he had anything that needed doing. Unfortunately, he had little to offer, but he did manage to open two beers, and he asked whether I had visited Franz Fitz yet. I apologised that I hadn't, but if I'm honest, at that time of my life I was a little shy about taking Franz Fitz up on his offer of just popping in to visit him.

Franz picked up the phone and called Franz Fitz. I could just about make out what the conversation was about, discussing what work Franz Fitz needed carrying out and that I could go over to see him to discuss the work in detail. He put the phone down and told me I was due to meet Franz Fitz the following day at 9am at his business premises on the other side of the city, where he would run through the work he would like me to do.

That evening was yet another on which I was thanking my buddy Franz, even if it did lead once again to another long evening of drinking beer and, on this occasion, whisky. Finally, in the late evening I was taking the short stagger home to see the boys safely into bed and to find Vanessa shaking her head once again at my usual lack of willpower!

The next morning, with a thick head and an awful taste in my mouth from the evening before, I arrived on time to see Franz Fitz. He spoke extremely clearly and slowly to me, ensuring that I could understand him. He nicknamed me 'mein meister' (my craftsman) from that moment on. The term was his way of calling me his master of roofing, and it was to stick with me throughout our relationship for years to come.

He walked me around the huge estate of several large buildings that made up his caravan and mobile home sales and rental business. Entering the large building to the entrance area, he explained that this was the first building he had bought when he started the business many years before. It contained several inflatable ribbed boats as well as a selection of sailing items, such as life jackets, ropes, small inflatable dinghies, as well as a selection of clothing, which all appeared to be expensive.

To my right was the caravan and mobile home shop, packed with rows of items that you might need to help to repair or improve your caravan or mobile home. You could change a door knob, install new windows or even a fully automatic television antenna.

On the first floor, the room to the left was packed with scores of bicycles, which Franz explained was his hobby. He picked them up from boot sales or from friends, then restored them in his spare time. I guess there must have been in excess of one hundred and fifty bikes in the room at all stages of repair and refurbishment, some in pieces and others in new working order. The one thing that was clear was that it would take an extremely long time to fulfil his hobby or dream of getting them all working again.

On the other side of the first floor was stock for the shop, but old stock at that. Most if not all of this area was full of material that had been boxed and stored for years, if not decades. Franz explained that he would try to sell this old stock one day, that he couldn't bring himself to throw it away, so had to store it until he could eventually sell it. As I would find out in the coming years, this room only ever housed more stock, and I don't think the old stock level ever dropped – it just grew over time.

The second floor of the building was inside the roof. This floor had three large dormer windows either side providing lots of natural light to the building. This was where Franz stored any old junk from days gone by, as well as his company records. Each year's trading records were stored on the endless purpose-built shelving.

Franz explained that the roof coverings here had never been repaired and he wanted me to inspect the whole roof. The six windows in the roof were covered with zinc, heavily rusted and in need of updating. He was open to suggestions but was happy to leave it to me to carry out whatever I thought was needed.

The next building we visited had large sliding doors that were almost two storeys high. It took both of us to slide one door open to gain access. Inside was a treasure trove of antique cars and motorbikes, including an early Porsche and three Mercedes Benz cars, one of which was a convertible. I later discovered that this was a Mercedes-Benz 280 SE, a car that to this day I would love to own, but alas my dream is still unfulfilled.

Franz also had cars from most periods of the twentieth century. One that surprised me was an early Mk1 BMW. It was the first time I had seen one, and although it looked very similar to the Mk2 that I remembered seeing during my childhood in the 1970s, this one was completely new to me. With its small round rear light cluster, distinct BMW body shape, with front chrome grill, it resembled an adult-sized Hillman Imp. Still to this day it's the only time I've ever seen one.

Franz told me that the oldest car in the building was under a protective cover. He carefully pulled the cover away to reveal his pride and joy, a Peugeot 402 vintage car in grey. Its wheels were painted red and, to me, it was the ugliest car I had ever seen. It must have been one of the very early cars that Citroën would later model their famous 2CV on, which was also ugly but had a huge cult following of buyers all over the world.

As well as his cars, Franz had several vintage motor bikes and scooters. Now I'm no expert on either but having ridden scooters in my teenage years there was one in the building that interested me, although I had no idea of its make. Franz told me it was a German-built scooter, an NSU

Prima 175cc that he'd had since his early days before his marriage. He had used the scooter to travel to his job but now it was in need of some TLC. However, it was by no means a rust bucket. It was a light green colour with a huge headlight and was to me the best thing I had seen that day so far. I couldn't imagine what the value of Franz's collection was, but the old shed it was stored in had no lock or security to it.

Franz also wanted me to carry out repair work to this building but explained that it would need to be emptied prior to any work being carried to ensure that the vehicles weren't damaged. He also thought it would be a good idea, as the building was of timber construction, that we give the whole place a good coat or two of timber preservative. That way he might, as he put it, get enough use out of the building in his lifetime.

The final building that we visited that day stood almost hidden behind a row of tall conifer trees and an enormous parking area full of motor homes and caravans. This building had been converted over time to become Franz's retirement house. I knew he was separated from his wife, even though she still worked at the place and they got on like a house on fire.

He walked me into the shell of the building. It wasn't massive like the previous two buildings but it would make a great property for him when finished. The inside was already fitted out and the walls, plaster boarding, electrics and plumbing were already in place. The kitchen had also been installed, along with two bathrooms, one upstairs and one downstairs. This had been his project for the past four years, carrying out most of the work himself with some help from friends and the occasional professional to install the electrics and plumbing.

Franz suggested that if the weather was wet outside or prevented me from working on the other buildings, I would be able to carry on working inside the new house. I could be decorating or helping him to carry on with the floors, as well as finishing the tiling to the two bathrooms. There was a whole heap of work, and with the three buildings to work on, I knew that if I played my cards right and looked after Franz, I could be working here every weekend for years.

I spent several hours with Franz walking around the place, just trying to understand the scale of the business he had built. Just prior to leaving, he reminded me that he would keep me busy here on site, but at certain times I would need to accompany him to his wife's or daughter's properties to carry out some roof repairs there as both had problems with water ingress.

This was just too good to be true. When I arrived home and explained to Vanessa exactly what had happened that morning, she too thought we had won the jackpot. We agreed that my buddy down the road, Franz, who had recommended my services, would be in for a big thank you.

The introduction to Franz Fitz would prove to be a huge help to our finances. I would work for him in one way or another for over three years. His wife lived in a lovely small property not far from the business, and she kept her car in a large block of twelve garages in one long row. I also ended up replacing the flat roof to all twelve of these garages after

Franz organised a great price with all the owners as long as they had the work carried out at the same time.

He just couldn't stop helping me and my family, and he even called upon the services of Thomas and Goran from time to time. I remember when Goran helped me on one occasion by securing the rope I was harnessed to inside the large three-floor main building. If I had a problem, he would be there to help me or call for help. The most memorable bit of working with Goran on the harness was when he asked if he could carry out some repairs as he had never been on a pitched roof before, and he wanted to learn a few new skills. We changed places and it turned out to be a complete disaster straight away. He had only just got outside one of the roof windows that we were using for access to the roof when he tried to stand up and I ended up having to grab hold of him quickly, as he completely went into meltdown with a fear of heights. He was used to working on flat roofs only. What was his first time on a pitched roof would undoubtedly also be his last, having taken several minutes to get on the roof and over forty minutes to get back off.

Thomas was fine on the pitched roof though, and he spent many a weekend helping when I was in need of another pair of hands. However, each day we worked there always finished the same way. Franz would have his barbeque fired up, an open metal grated fire, with a steel shelf sitting over the top, and he would be cooking bratwurst. He had long wooden skewers sticking into the end of them so that we could pick them up to eat when cooked. The beer was always Zwiefalter Klosterbräu, and many an evening was spent sharing a beer and sausage before heading home.

We got paid at the end of every day. Franz Fitz paid by the hour, and he always asked that we inform him when we arrived so that he knew when we started work. Regardless of what happened throughout the day, he would always pay us for every hour, even the hour or so we were eating sausage with him and enjoying a beer. He was such a lovely kind man, and I have such fond memories of those years, with the many weekends spent sharing a cold beer with him around those open fires while he cooked the sausages.

My dream car ... Mercedes-Benz 280 SE convertible

Peugeot 402 – Franz's baby

The ugly Citroen 2CV

Franz's beloved NSU Prima 175cc scooter

Chapter 19

Euro '96 ... Verdient und Verloren

WITH FOOTBALL being probably the most important part of my sons' lives by this time, like all football fanatics they will always remember their first European Championships and World Cup. It's a time when you begin to really understand the football world continentally and globally. It's also a time when lifelong allegiances are formed as you take pride in your national colours and team. We all heed the do-or-die call to urge our nation on to victory or, if you're English, picking up the pieces and telling everyone that we were robbed ... again.

England were hosting the European Championships in 1996 and the whole country was crazy with football fever. Approaching the tournament there was a new football anthem being played daily across the whole of Europe. It was on every European radio station, not just in the UK, including in Germany. 'Three Lions' was that anthem, which is still sung today by every nation, particularly the catchy line, 'Football's coming home.'

During Euro '96, this was the will of the English nation, singing together, all enjoying the journey with the team and a hope, yes maybe even the dream, that this time was our time. The tournament was on home soil and if England had that little bit of luck that every team needs they could finally lift the trophy and be champions of Europe, bringing the spoils home just as this anthem to football suggests.

Leading up to the event, the boys and their friends from their football teams had all been discussing the tournament. Who would win? How good are Germany? Being English there was no need to ask who my boys' favourite team was, or to ask who was going to win. Terry Venables was going to bring some silverware back to the nation after 'thirty years of hurt', another line from 'Three Lions'.

With players such as Paul 'Gazza' Gascoigne, who was at his mercurial best, Alan Shearer, Stuart 'Psycho' Pearce, Paul Ince, and with the great David Seaman in goal, England were a team to be reckoned with and the anthem took the nation and the squad to a new level of expectation. It had the same impact on us expats living in Reutlingen, flying the English flag for our home nation.

Thomas was naturally backing Germany as you would expect, and Goran was right behind the Croatian team, who against the odds had qualified for the final stages. His dream was to beat the Germans in the semi-finals and then England in the final. In fact, work was great for the whole three weeks of the tournament. We had football on the radio most days and when Germany, Croatia or England were due to play we would down tools, have an early finish if needed and get home in time to watch the matches.

The opening match of the tournament was England versus Switzerland. The home nation was expected to win comfortably but only managed a disappointing 1-1 draw. Alan Shearer put England into the lead midway through the first half, but the Swiss equalised through a penalty with seven minutes of the match remaining.

I was at home with all three boys watching this first match. Their faces were painted with the England red and white of the St George cross, and they were loving the football. Gernold was with us to watch the match too, although we couldn't persuade him to have his face painted. This wasn't the dream start the nation or we had hoped for but at least we hadn't lost. The other two teams in the group, Scotland and the Netherlands played out a goalless draw two days later, so it was all still to play for to qualify from the group stage, with the top two going through to the knockout rounds.

The day after England's match, the German football machine, as expected, won their first match against the Czech Republic, 2-0. This was an easy opener for them against a poor team, so there was plenty of good banter from me and Goran at work, letting Thomas know that Germany had only won due to the poor opposition. Then when Croatia played their first match a couple of days later, it took a goal in the last five minutes to break the deadlock against a stubborn Turkey. It was Croatia's first win at a European Championship finals.

Next up for England was a match against the 'auld enemy' Scotland, one that would elevate the English national team and Gazza into delirium. It was 15 June and the sky was clear and blue on a warm day at Wembley. Meanwhile, in Reutlingen, my family again had their faces painted. Gernold was with us, as well as Karl-Heinz and Julian, twins and school friends of Sam and Jake. These two also had their faces painted with the English flag, and their parents had come round to watch the match, despite not really knowing the first thing about football. But they were here to support England and help cheer our team on to victory.

Both teams were naturally fired up by the historical significance of the match. England needed to establish their worth at Euro '96 after their disappointing draw in the opener, while Scotland had excelled and were full of confidence after their draw against the world-class Dutch team. The match today was due to be a classic, and the next ninety minutes would be a roller coaster that we would all savour.

Our front room was buzzing with anticipation, with a house full of children who all loved football. Us adults had a few beers flowing, but not too many. However, the first half turned out to be eventless, with maybe Scotland having the better of it as England appeared to be scared of losing and perhaps not playing with enough freedom.

Nevertheless, the boys were all having fun and were enjoying the atmosphere. It was lovely to see their smiling faces and all their friends helping to cheer on England to hopefully win. They spent most of the half-time break discussing why England weren't winning and what they thought the second half would bring. There was even a very odd suggestion that England should ask Klinsmann to turn up to help them for the second half. After a bit of a giggle, I had to explain why that could never happen.

At the start of the second half England brought on Jamie Redknapp, a player I really rated, and only eight minutes later he was involved in a move that resulted in Gary Neville crossing for Alan Shearer to open the scoring with a header. Shearer's arm was aloft in his usual style and the front room was in chaos, with children and adults jumping with glee as we celebrated the opening goal. Vanessa was playing the 'Three Lions' anthem as loud as she could get it on a tape recorder, and we were singing as proud Englishmen and ladies (with a few German infiltrators).

Scotland weren't deterred by the goal though, and Gordon Durie soon forced a great save from Seaman in the England goal. Then, five minutes later, Durie was fouled in the penalty area by Tony Adams and the referee pointed to the spot. The boys were starting to feel what being an England fan is like, a feeling I was only too used to, with my many years of disappointment of watching England suffer defeat at tournaments.

Scotland's Gary McAllister, usually so reliable in a dead-ball situation, placed the ball on the penalty spot. The boys covered their eyes, unable watch. As McAllister approached to take his penalty kick, the ball moved slightly, but he continued his run-up and struck the ball. However, he placed it too close to Seaman in goal, who pulled off a relatively easy save. Our room erupted into euphoric cheers of joy.

From that moment on there was to be no further pain for England. Only ninety seconds later the ball reached Gazza, who ran at the Scottish defence, entering the penalty box as the ball was bouncing. What followed was a piece of perfect artistry, as Gazza simply lobbed the ball over the static centre-back, Colin Hendry, then struck the ball on the volley past Andy Goram in the Scotland goal for 2-0, a lead that England held on to for the remaining eleven minutes.

I'm not sure whether it was Wembley that could be heard from Reutlingen or whether Reutlingen could be heard at Wembley, but either way this was an England victory that would be remembered in our household for years to come. It was a victory that I'm sure everyone in the room that day has the same wonderful memories of, our nation dreaming of future glory. On the final whistle Vanessa had the anthem blaring out again, so all the neighbourhood knew the English had won and we were all making the best of this great victory.

The following day the whole house was still buzzing. On the same day, Germany breezed past Russia 3-0, while Croatia beat Denmark 3-0, so both teams topped their respective groups and had already secured their places in the knockout stage. However, England still had some work to do as they now had a tough match against the Netherlands and needed a victory to be certain of qualification. So, it was my turn to get some stick from Thomas and Goran, who were ribbing me about how difficult it was going to be for England.

England's final group match was in the evening, but we let the three boys stay up, even though it was an 8.30pm kick-off in local time. It was to be a match in which England played in the style normally associated with their opposition. The Netherlands had absolutely no answer to England's fantastic display. Football really came home in the most stunning style that night, with what became known as

GERMANY – IT'S MORE THAN BRATWURST & WEISSBIER

England's SAS (Shearer and Sheringham) dream team scoring twice each.

Given England's performances in the previous two matches, there was a genuine nervousness ahead of the Netherlands match; however, Terry Venables and his team turned English football on its head on this night. Not only did the Three Lions hammer world-class opposition, but they scored a perfect ten for artistic impression as well. The lasting memories for me were the runs of Gazza and the performance of Teddy Sheringham, who was untouchable.

Meanwhile, Alan Shearer's two goals meant he was now the leading scorer in the tournament. England had qualified as the group winners but were now in for a tough quarter-final against Spain. However, at this stage, who cared?

The following evening after I arrived home from work, I went with the boys to the local park to play out the England match from the previous evening. The park was full of children playing football and they all wanted to be on the England team. It was a struggle to get anyone to be on the Netherlands team, so we decided everyone would take turns at playing on each team – everyone except the three young English boys and their dad of course.

That evening was the start of weeks of football for us as a family. All the local children wanted to play for England. They had all seen a world-class team move the ball like Brazilians as we took the Dutch to pieces, so why wouldn't any German youngster want to be English and follow the dream?

In their final group match, Germany drew 0-0 with Italy to go through as group winners, but Croatia lost to Portugal, who topped the group, so Croatia qualified as runners-up. This meant that Germany and Croatia were matched against each other in the quarter-finals, in what would be not only a winner takes all on the field but would also provide bragging rights at work. We also knew that whoever won that match would face the winners of the England versus Spain match, so it was all to play for.

England played first, an afternoon match, and the face paint was out again. We also had some fizzy drinks and Dickmann's on the table, as we all viewed in expectation of an England win, which would take them into the semi-finals. However, after all the excitement of the matches against Scotland and the Netherlands, the quarter-final was one to forget.

England had Seaman to thank again, as his saves prevented Spain winning in the regulation ninety minutes. The match went into extra time. This tournament was using the much-maligned 'golden goal' system, which meant that whoever scored first in extra time was the winner. However, the additional thirty minutes failed to produce a goal, so the match would be decided on penalties, not England's strong point.

We were all watching in disbelief at the poor England performance today, and my boys hadn't shown the same enthusiasm as they had for the three previous matches. And with a penalty shootout to come, I feared the worst, as I had never seen England win a shootout, and the omens weren't good, given such a poor performance so far in the match.

Spain took the first penalty and missed, so our front room erupted as we all cheered their failure to score. Alan

Shearer stepped up, and I just couldn't watch, but the boys had no fear as they watched him blast the ball home for a 1-0 lead. Both teams then scored their next two penalties. For England, the first was scored by David Platt, then one of my all-time favourite players, Stuart Pearce, stepped up.

'Psycho' had missed his crucial penalty in the 1990 World Cup semi-final shootout against Germany, but here he drilled the ball home with aplomb, following up with a magnificent fist-pumping to the crowd, as the veins stood out on his face and neck. For me it was a great feeling of triumph to see him score, and it was a day for him to wipe out the memory of his previous miss. England now led 3-2 in the shootout after three spot kicks each.

Even better was to follow when Spain missed for the second time. This was turning into a dream, as England were now on the verge of winning the match, as long as Gazza could score with the next penalty. We were quiet now, and even Vanessa was nervous as Gazza stepped up. But he didn't let us down, scoring to give England a 4-2 victory in this cruellest form of football.

We, however, didn't care how cruel it was, as we were back in full song. England were into the semi-finals of the European Championship. We may have been hanging on at times against Spain but we weren't bothered by that. 'Three Lions' rang out once again that night as we celebrated together.

The following day was Germany versus Croatia, and it was Germany who came away victorious, 2-1, after a hard-fought match. It was a win that gave them a place in their sixth European semi-final. Jürgen Klinsmann's penalty had put Germany ahead but a Davor Šuker goal just after half-time levelled things up. Matthias Sammer then put Germany back in front, a lead they held on to for the victory.

Croatia would have to settle for the fact that they had outplayed Germany, at times having them on the back foot. In fact, Germany were there for the taking following Šuker's equaliser. However, a red card for Štimac halted Croatia in their tracks. They had shown themselves to be nothing if not resilient and Goran was immensely proud of his nation's first appearance in a major tournament. I had to admit that the Germans were extremely lucky in managing to scrape through this close-fought contest, but now they were heading for the semi-final meeting with England.

Wednesday, 26 June 1996
Euro '96 semi-final
England vs Germany

England was, once again, a nation of hope. The Three Lions were taking on the might of the Germans in what promised to be a Wembley Stadium classic. Once again, we were face-painted and we had home-made England flags hanging from the ceiling. The boys were wearing England football shirts received from their grandparents, Diane and Jock, and were buzzing like never before.

This was England's opportunity to show just how good they had become. Our neighbours and their children were with us today, but of course the German children had their faces painted in the red, black and gold of their national flag. But this was party time for everyone, all hoping and praying for the win for their respective team.

It was another 8.30pm kick-off, and when the referee started the match everyone began to cheer. With only three minutes on the clock, England were ahead through an Alan Shearer header. Our German visitors suddenly went very quiet. This was for them the worst possible start, but not for me and my three young English lions. We hit the roof, jumping and cheering on our team, and Lee charged around the front room with his arm held high, à la Shearer.

It really was one of the most emotional few minutes of my life when we took the lead, and I could feel the tears welling up inside me. But the elation didn't last long, as within fifteen minutes the scores were level when Stefan Kuntz snuck through England's defence to score. This time it was the English in the room who were dejected, going from feeling so high to being so, so low in such a short time. Of course, we had to suffer the celebrations of our German friends and neighbours too.

From that moment on it was a tense, tactical battle between two top-quality teams but there was no addition to the score and the match went into extra time. Not one of the children were tired though, all hanging on to the highs and lows suffered by both teams as the final whistle went.

Both teams had good chances to score in extra time, with Darren Anderton denied by the woodwork. We were already cheering in anticipation of the goal that never was. Germany then had a goal controversially disallowed … well, when I say controversially, with a room that included our German friends and children, all adamant the goal was good, then, on the other hand, the English contingent convinced the goal had been rightly ruled out, it was definitely controversial in our house.

With just a few minutes remaining before the dreaded penalty shootout, Teddy Sheringham pushed the ball wide to England's right to Shearer, who drove in a low ball across the German goal area. The German keeper and defenders couldn't get a touch on the ball, and suddenly there was Gazza steaming in at the far post. Surely the nation's hero was going to slide in to take the glory and score the winning 'golden goal'. All he had to do was get a touch on the ball, any touch ... he couldn't miss.

We all screamed at him ... begging him to put the ball into the net ... but it didn't happen. Despite Gazza's desperate lunge and his outstretched leg, he couldn't quite get to the ball in time and missed it by millimetres. Shortly after this, the final whistle went and England were into another penalty shootout with Germany to decide a place in the final.

The tension in the room was unbearable and everyone was on edge. My boys were confident England would win after having beaten Spain on penalties in the last round. The tension then mounted even further as both teams successfully converted their penalties to leave the score at 5-5, which meant it was now sudden death.

England were going first and it was future national team manager, a young Gareth Southgate, who stepped up. To the England supporters' dismay, he hit a very tame effort that was easily saved by Köpke in the German goal. It was now down to our own keeper, David Seaman, to keep the nation's dream alive. Unfortunately, Andreas Möller took an inch-perfect penalty and Seaman was easily beaten.

England had lost again to Germany in a penalty shootout and were out of the tournament.

The English fans in our room fell into silence with utter dejection and, of course, our German friends celebrated their victory. The rest of the night was to me a blur, and everyone left to go home after a late finish to the match. It was almost midnight and this household was going to bed broken-hearted.

At work the following day I was greeted by Thomas and Goran. Thomas told me that the match was 'verdient und verloren', which means 'earned and lost'. It was little consolation, but I would hear this saying for weeks to come from almost every German I met ... you had earned the win but you lost it. It was a hard ending to a few weeks of a great tournament, especially having shared it with my boys, watching every match and loving every minute of the journey.

The final was played the following Sunday, and Franz threw a huge barbeque, with a large-screen TV set up so everyone could enjoy a great afternoon and evening with family and friends. Germany scraped a 2-1 win with a 'golden goal' against the Czech Republic, so it was the boys' hero Jürgen Klinsmann who lifted the trophy. The rest, shall we say, is history, regardless of how many times I would be told that England had 'verdient und verloren'.

Chapter 20

Meeting Mr Knoll

IT WAS early autumn and life was getting back to normal now that we had stopped playing England versus Germany in the local park with the local children. On some evenings we had been joined by a few of the fathers and by now my shins were sore after taking so many kicks from them.

My job was going well and we were working in the local region on a development of four apartment blocks, each block with thirty-two apartments and each having at least one large terrace. We had work enough to see us through the next four to six weeks.

Our previous job had meant being away from home for three weeks, not that we needed to be away as it wasn't that far from Reutlingen. However, the hitch was that we were working on a new roof installation on an electrical plant that was starting the close-down of one of its two nuclear reactors, with the nuclear waste being moved from site to the UK for its disposal. This fact hadn't gone unnoticed in the UK, and there were demonstrations held to vent people's anger.

The plant had a direct docking facility on the river Necker, which allowed barges to remove waste from the facility. It also had a rail link running through the plant for extraction of material, not forgetting the normal road links that allowed the waste to be moved from the plant every week. The main problem was that it was never disclosed whether the waste was going to be shipped by road, rail or river. So, each time a waste delivery was leaving the plant, there were several lorries with a police and army escort, the railway had a train leaving from site, as well as a large barge on the river also giving the illusion of waste being on it.

The company was cleverly using all three systems to disguise the fact that only they knew which system would be carrying the nuclear waste. So, with all this going on, we were right in the middle of it all installing a new roof covering. It was agreed that it would be easier for us to stay on site rather than trying to get home through the demonstrations, where there could be up to five thousand people.

This meant we were being paid for our eight-hour shift, plus for a sixteen-hour day away from our homes. We also finished the job two weeks early, so with the extra money we were being paid and the time saved on our fixed-price period, we had a huge bonus due, which came out at almost six weeks' wages each.

After finishing at the electrical plant, back in Reutlingen we were having a slow week on our new job. However, with our bonus from the previous job coming at the end of the month, we could afford to have an easy week on this job. When payday arrived, I was over the moon, although I did have to pay a lot of tax. However, the take-home pay was almost three times my usual basic pay, so for a three-week job it had turned out to be a real good earner.

We didn't normally discuss our wages at work. I always feel it's a personal issue for each employee. Thomas, though, couldn't hold back on the fact he had received a bonus payment, which gave him a two-week bonus after tax on his basic pay. I realised that something wasn't right in what he said, so during our breakfast break that day I asked him whether he could explain his bonus, as it wasn't the same as mine.

Thomas explained it again and it transpired that he hadn't had a bonus payment that gave him three times his normal pay like I had received, but only two weeks' basic payment as a bonus. Given this apparent mistake in Thomas's pay, I asked Goran what his payment was. The answer I received was totally unexpected, as Goran explained that it didn't matter what overtime he worked or how many hours were gained as bonus from our price work, he only ever received his basic pay. Always had done. At no time since we had all been together over the previous two years had he ever received any bonus payment in his wage packet.

I was completely numb. This was a young man who had never said no to working late or when I insisted he worked Saturdays so that we could increase our bonus payments. He was always there, always working hard, never complaining, and never had he mentioned money or a lack of it.

Over the course of the day as we laboured with little enthusiasm, I was starting to realise that it was only me who had actually received the full bonus payment due to us. Thomas had received only a percentage and Goran had received nothing. This was unjust and I knew that it needed to be addressed, but first I needed to understand how I could do this in such a way that we all got our money, while not ending up losing or jobs over it.

I discussed it with Vanessa that evening and she was just as horrified as me at the way that Goran and Thomas had been treated. I was adamant that I would leave over this if necessary. How could I continue to work for an employer who treated their workers with such disregard? This was a blatant violation of employment law in my eyes. However, I needed to calm down.

There's a good reason I share almost everything with Vanessa – because she has a level head, while I see the red mist. She has a way of calming the situation and making me see the light and reasoning behind the problem at hand. This was another of those occasions.

She reminded me that if I was to turn the clock back almost six months, I had been on a project in Neu Ulm, a huge shopping centre. We weren't the only roofing company on the project and I had been approached by the manager of the other company, a gentleman called Mr Knoll. I didn't know how he knew me but he had addressed me as Martin when he approached me to talk on site. It turned out it was a relation of Thomas who had previously worked for Mr Knoll who had given him my details.

Mr Knoll seemingly knew all about me and the projects I had worked on. Although at that stage he didn't make a direct approach to employ me, he gave me his business card, and his parting comment was that there was a door always open for good guys like me. Vanessa now pulled out his business card and suggested it might be good to first have a chat with him, just to see what opportunities might be available for me and the guys.

So, the following day I talked with Goran and Thomas, and we all agreed that I would contact Mr Knoll. We were hoping to get an interview to discuss the possibility of a move to his company as a group, not individually, and see what that package would be. If we could get that sorted, we could then approach Herr Schmitt, our current employer, to address the situation regarding Thomas and Goran, knowing we had a job to go to if things didn't go well with that conversation.

I called Mr Knoll that evening but got only his answer machine, so I did no more than leave my first name and my phone number, with no explanation of what I wanted to talk about. About two hours later the phone rang and it was Herr Knoll, who knew exactly who I was from my English accent on the message I had left. He spoke almost no English, but I asked if it was possible to meet him to discuss the possibility of a position for three of us with his company. He explained that we would have to wait for a week due to the fact that he was going on holiday with his family the following day, but he would meet us on his return.

The following day, I explained the situation to Thomas and Goran. It was another week of waiting, but it was a small price to pay to try to find a solution to this problem. It seemed a long week too, and our production on site wasn't up to our normal standard, as none of us had any enthusiasm for the job.

On the following Monday evening, Mr Knoll called and asked to meet on the Thursday evening at his regional office in Neckartenzlingen. However, I was to go alone as he wanted to discuss this with me only. When I told the others the following day they weren't too pleased but they trusted me to do the right thing.

This week seemed to go quicker and Thursday soon came around. I was a bit late for the meeting with Mr Knoll as I had taken twenty minutes to find his office, so I was feeling a little stressed when I walked in. I was greeted by Herr Knoll, who was drinking coffee and smoking a cigarette. He made me coffee and I accepted a cigarette, as we sat and talked about the possibility of us moving to work for him.

It was clear to me that we were wanted by him, even more than we wanted to move to him. Over the next hour and a half I negotiated an offer for the three of us that would see us all receive an improvement in our wages. We were guaranteed not to be working away from home and all jobs would be price work, the way we had worked for the past year. Holiday entitlements were the same as our existing job, as well as bank holidays, but we would get an additional holiday bonus payment of 25 per cent of our wages, given to us in cash on the last day before our main summer and Christmas holidays. This was to be on top of any bonus moneys we had earned.

This package was a good one and the lads were happy with the deal when I explained it to them the following day. All we needed now was the employment contracts to arrive, then we could deal with Mr Schmitt. We still hoped we wouldn't need to move jobs, that Mr Schmitt would see sense and pay Thomas and Goran their back-payment of bonus and give them an apology.

All three employment contracts arrived at my home two weeks later. It was a Friday so we had the weekend to sit on them. I called into Mr Schmitt's office first thing Monday morning to ask for a meeting and he told me to come back after work as he had a busy start to the week.

I returned in the evening as asked, while Thomas and Goran waited downstairs. It was a difficult situation; he could see no problem with the fact that Goran hadn't been paid any bonuses during his time working in the company.

'He's a Yugo!' were his exact words, followed by, 'He's lucky to have a job.'

Mr Schmitt showed no interest in Thomas's situation either and couldn't see why I thought it so wrong. His attitude was that I had been paid my bonuses so I should forget about the others. I found this situation stressful, so after almost half an hour I made it very clear that if the situation wasn't resolved today there would be no option but for us to leave to try to find other employment.

Obviously I didn't mention the offer we had already received but I made it clear that I appreciated everything he had done for me personally during my time with the company, but this was a matter of principle and I wouldn't be able to carry on working there unless Goran and Thomas were treated equally with their bonus payments. Mr Schmitt told me to sleep on it. He thought it a rash decision to offer our resignations en masse over this, and he asked me to return to see him the following evening to discuss it further.

That evening I discussed the outcome of the meeting with Goran and Thomas. We knew the choice that was in our hands: we could go to Mr Knoll, make a fresh start with everything on the table as had been agreed, or hold out in the hope that Mr Schmitt would change his mind. We were all in agreement that if Schmitt hadn't changed his mind by the morning, we would all walk, and take the new position with Knoll. Why should we waste such an opportunity in the hope that Mr Schmitt might change his ways?

The three of us arrived early for work the next morning, and this time we all entered Mr Schmitt's office as I didn't want there to be any misunderstandings. This had to be everyone's choice if we left, not just mine. However, Mr Schmitt's mind on this was the same as the day before. He apologised to Goran and Thomas, but as far as he was concerned, he had delivered everything they were entitled to.

I had heard enough, so I stood up and shook his hand, thanked him for the time he had employed me and gave him my resignation and notice period of fourteen days. Thomas did the same, followed by Goran. Mr Schmitt looked shell-shocked, and it was obvious that he thought we were calling his bluff and had no intention of leaving. But now we had done it and I knew there was to be no return for me. I turned and walked, and the lads followed me, while Mr Schmitt was shouting at me that I would regret this, that it was okay for me to leave but I shouldn't take his workers too. He accused me of breaking his trust and told me there would be no return after this.

I felt relieved as we left work that evening. There was a pressure removed. As neither Thomas nor Goran had received their proper bonus payments, over the coming two weeks we decided to work to rule, just turning up and plodding through the days.

During our final week, all three of us were due two days' holiday, so the Wednesday would be our last day. On that morning, Mr Schmitt called us into his office and asked whether we could work our holidays as they were extremely busy. It was a unanimous decision to this question ... it's a no from me, him and him. With that we turned and walked out of his office to start our last day.

The following Monday we started working for Mr Knoll. New company, new life to lead, but the same work team. We were to have lots more adventures together in the coming years.

That, however, would take me so much more time to put pen to paper, but maybe one day I will ...

Epilogue

I WAS 23 years of age when the wall fell in the old East Germany in 1989, and I had no idea this would be so influential in my life and my family's future. Just over twelve months later I would be making my way through Germany, leaving my family life behind, rebuilding my career in search of a well-paid job, as I played my part in the rebuilding of the 'new' Germany.

It would be another eighteen months before Vanessa and the boys joined me in Reutlingen, agreeing to stay for a minimum of six months to see how it worked out. Vanessa had had to put up with living and coping without me for so long while I was in Germany, with infrequent visits from me and no mobile phones. She also had to deal with the added pressure of repaying the debts that had been accrued from the losses of my company.

Their arrival in Germany provided us the opportunity to rebuild our family life together. I can't say that it was easy those first few months, but after the six months' trial period, as I plucked up courage to ask Vanessa whether she wanted to return to the UK, I was really dreading the answer.

It turned out I was worrying over nothing, as she had fallen in love with the local people, our lovely neighbours, the customs and this new culture we were experiencing. And all three of our sons had been given an opportunity – one that few children get offered in life – to experience new cultures, learn new languages and explore the world from a young age.

Almost thirty years on, I've looked back on this time with fond memories. Although some of the experiences were stressful at the time, most were wonderful and have enriched our lives individually and as a family. Our life in Germany has not only made me the man I am today but has shaped my wonderful wife's life just the same way.

As our sons grew up, they all went on to travel much more than Vanessa and I ever did. They had seen the world far and wide by the time they were all twenty-five years of age, which is something I'm extremely proud of. Those years in Germany were the start of a life we would all live in different countries, exploring different cultures.

Maybe one day I'll carry on and document some more of these experiences of our time in Germany, but I want to tell you that you don't need to have a well-paid job to work and live abroad. As I did back then, you just need dedication and a drive to succeed. When others sat and admitted failure and defeat, I was traveling into Europe, with Germany seeming to be a million miles away. These days it's just a ninety-minute flight.

I kept going, eventually succeeding, but not to prove my doubters wrong or to have the best-paid job on offer. I paid my debts and won the jackpot. I was one part of the rebuilding of our family, a life that without Vanessa and her endless support, wouldn't have been possible.

We have subsequently built a lifetime of memories together, something no one can ever take away from us, all five of us. We're still happily married and still moving countries. The boys are growing up and building families of their own, probably the biggest measure of success that both Vanessa and I share today.

I hope you enjoyed reading about our journey.
Auf wiedersehen.

The apartment house we lived in pictured here in 2019. We lived in the ground floor apartment behind the parked car.

Reutlingen, with the Achalm mountain in the background

Main shopping street in Reutlingen

Reutlingen Cathedral

Fortifications gateway around the old city of Reutlingen

Acknowledgements

Writing isn't something that comes naturally to me. I've taken to writing now that I've retired and it keeps me busy and in a good routine after years of building businesses and working all the hours I could. My life is a little less hectic now and the one thing I do have is time. Time to enjoy with my lovely wife Vanessa, who as always looks after me and ensures that I stay grounded in whatever I do.

Once again, she has encouraged me to put pen to paper, this time documenting our early years while living in Germany. I'm also sure that now the book is finished, she and my three sons will enjoy these memories for many years to come. If they get half the enjoyment from reading the book that I've had writing it, then I'm sure they will enjoy reliving the memories that we all share. Without such a lovely close family, none of this would have been possible.

I'm what can only be described as a professional dreamer. I hold a first-class honours in it, but without Vanessa's help and being there to steer me through life and rein me in on the odd occasion, those dreams would, I'm sure, amount to very little. So, I thank her for being who she is and helping me to be who I am.

I thank you Vanessa with all my heart xx

A Final Note

I'm a self-publishing author who thrives on receiving reviews of the work I publish. I would love to read a review from you, my reader. Don't worry if you feel you need to be critical, as my skin is very thick. I enjoy reading all constructive criticism and it really is the very best part of the book once I've finished and published it online.

If you have any further questions or comments that you would like to ask me personally, please feel free to contact me, Martin Barber, at the following email address:

martindbarber66@gmail.com

Thank you, Martin

Not forgetting!!

I would also like to mention my editor, Ivan. Without him the book really wouldn't be in any condition to read, so thank you Ivan. I've once again invited him to include his business details here, just in case you read this book, are then inspired to write your own journey and need a good editor.

Ivan Butler MBA – Coachhouse Business Services

Copy-editing & Proofreading Professional

Email: ivanbutler897@btinternet.com

www.coachhousebusinessservices.co.uk

Printed in Great Britain
by Amazon